AIR CAMPAIGN

HAMBURG 1940–45

The long war against Germany's great port city

RICHARD WORRALL | ILLUSTRATED BY MADS BANGSØ

OSPREY PUBLISHING
Bloomsbury Publishing Plc
Kemp House, Chawley Park, Cumnor Hill, Oxford OX2 9PH, UK
29 Earlsfort Terrace, Dublin 2, Ireland
1385 Broadway, 5th Floor, New York, NY 10018, USA
E-mail: info@ospreypublishing.com
www.ospreypublishing.com

OSPREY is a trademark of Osprey Publishing Ltd

First published in Great Britain in 2024

A catalogue record for this book is available from the British Library.

ISBN: PB 9781472859280; eBook 9781472859303;
ePDF 9781472859297; XML 9781472859310

24 25 26 27 28 10 9 8 7 6 5 4 3 2 1

Maps and diagrams by www.bounford.com
3D BEVs by Paul Kime
Index by Alan Rutter
Typeset by PDQ Digital Media Solutions, Bungay, UK
Printed and bound in India by Replika Press Private Ltd.

Title page: Please see caption on page 86.

Author's Note
The author would like to express
his gratitude to the team at Osprey
for turning plain – and frequently
overlength! Word documents into
this finished product, which has been
designed perfectly. Special mention
should be made to series editor Tom
Milner. I must also express thanks
to digital artist Mads Bangsø, the
map designers at Bounford, the BEV
illustrator Paul Kime, and diagram
drawer Adam Tooby for their extremely
vivid artwork and illustrations, and for
bringing this book to 'visual' life. Any
errors of fact and detail do, of course,
remain the author's responsibility.
Sincere thanks go to the staff at The
National Archives (Kew) and the
Library RAF Museum (Hendon),
Cristina Neagu at Christ Church Library
Archives (Oxford), the archivist team at
Churchill College Archives (Cambridge),
and the staff at the *Bundesarchiv*
(Koblenz). Kind permission was given
by Pen & Sword for the quotations from
the books by Guy Gibson, Arthur Harris
and Wilhelm Johnen. I would like to
dedicate this book to my parents, and
our PA from Leipzig.

CONTENTS

INTRODUCTION

'a general reduction in activity such as is known to have taken place in
U-boat construction is precisely the result which might be expected to
follow on the destruction of industrial centres and the disorganisation of
German production which has been the avowed aim of strategic bombing'

Air Chief Marshal Arthur 'Bomber' Harris, C-in-C Bomber Command,
7 March 1944

Within a week of Germany's surrender in May 1945, a Dakota transport aircraft took off
bound for Germany with a small party of Anglo-American airmen from the Combined
Strategic Targets Committee (CSTC) who were to see first hand the results of the Anglo-
American strategic bombing offensive against Germany's towns and cities. Having viewed
from the air the destruction at Hamburg, they landed at Lüneburg to take a car into the
city. Recording that 'the main features' at Hamburg were the flak towers and a civilian
population who still somehow lived amongst the ruins, often in wooden shacks, Air
Commodore Sydney Bufton (Director of Bomber Operations at the Air Ministry) recorded
they 'were greatly impressed by the extent of the damage' to the town and docks, whilst
that inflicted on the city's oil refineries 'was enormous'. 'Altogether,' Bufton informed an
American officer, 'the expedition was a fitting conclusion to the efforts of the CSTC.' What
Bufton and his colleagues, who also included the Marxist intellectual and future minister in
the post-war Labour Government, Air Commodore John Strachey, had witnessed was the
destruction caused by Bomber Command's air campaign against Hamburg, which had run
from 17–18 May 1940 to 13–14 April 1945. In total, Bomber Command dropped 22,580
tons on this great port city, a statistic ranking it fifth behind Berlin (45,517 tons), Essen
(36,420 tons), Cologne (34,711 tons) and Duisburg (30,025 tons), whilst the Americans
made numerous heavy attacks during 1944 and 1945. Yet the fiery raids of summer 1943
ensured the level of damage to Hamburg was particularly severe, the denouement of the

British conception of strategic bombing that had developed over several decades. On 15 June 1945, the RAF's 'founding father', Lord Trenchard, told an American friend: 'I have just come back from Germany where I saw the tremendous work the Air has done – it was terrific.' The Ruhr, Bremen and Hamburg showed 'how much the Air has done to win this war', 'Boom' Trenchard enthused.

Bomber Command's development as the true and devastating strategic bomber force it became, coupled with Hamburg's experience of bombing for nearly five years, means that in this book a longer view of the air campaign against Germany's second city has been taken. Existing accounts often focus solely on the destructive raids of July 1943 (Operation *Gomorrah*), but this book examines developments both before and after this period. Thus, the effort of Air Chief Marshal Sir Richard Peirse to assist the Battle of the Atlantic with 911 sorties made between January and June, often against Hamburg's shipyards, will be explored. So too will the attacks of 1944–45, when Hamburg was targeted because of its oil refineries and assembly of prefabricated U-boats. Naval and wider military considerations therefore form two important backstories in the bombing of Hamburg, alongside the development of area bombing and attacks on industrial workers. On 20 October 1943, Rear Admiral J.H. Edelsten told Bomber Command chief Arthur Harris that the bombing of Hamburg, together with a raid on Kiel on 4–5 April, showed 'the success' Bomber Command had made 'on our behalf to destroy U-boats'. Citing that it was 'a great achievement', Edelsten and the Naval Staff hoped Harris would 'find the opportunity completely to polish off Kiel'. Yet Harris' reply deliberately emphasized that bombing affected 'the enemy's war effort [generally]', not just U-boat production specifically. This reflected the war's middle years as being notable less for bombing precise industries than in attacking the morale and housing of the enemy's industrial workforce, the latter being targets fully conforming to the purists' concept of strategic bombing.

Only by making a full appreciation of Bomber Command's war against Hamburg can its development as a strategic bomber force be fully seen. '[N]ot until 1943', the Air Historical Branch (AHB) Narrative concludes, was 'the Command in a position to

The beautiful Hanseatic City of Hamburg in 1894. Here is the Lombard Bridge which crossed and divided the Alster Lakes – a key geographical reference point for Bomber Command's aircrews and their H2S device. (Getty Images)

The utter decimation of Hamburg's dock area seen from the destroyed oil-tank farm on the south bank of the Elbe. (Getty Images)

carry out its long planned policy of true strategic bombing; that is to say, the bombing of selected targets on a scale sufficient to break the industrial capacity and undermine the morale of the enemy'. Having developed steadily throughout 1942 in terms of quality if not quantity of the bombing force, with new devices, methods and techniques, Bomber Command, if by no means the complete package in early 1943, was sufficiently good to contemplate greater destruction throughout Germany generally, and to Hamburg specifically, over the forthcoming year. On 30 January 1943, Harris sent Robert Lovett, US Assistant Secretary of State for Air, a paper on the bombing results achieved in 1942. On Hamburg, 'no absolutely devastating results have been achieved', the C-in-C wrote, and 'it has yet to experience the results of a thoroughly successful mass attack'. This was soon set to change in July 1943.

Of course, the *Gomorrah* raids were undertaken alongside attacks made by the US VIII Bomber Command, Eighth Air Force. The American efforts, both during 1943 and later on, are certainly not neglected in this volume, but space limitations mean a detailed examination cannot be undertaken; this is really a subject for a volume on the US Eighth itself. Nonetheless, Hamburg contained specific war industries which they would attack, using their ideas of making precision attacks on vital industrial nodes and target sets, again and again. Thus, the contrasting approaches towards strategic bombing become markedly clear when examined through the example of Hamburg. Indeed, in July 1943, the Americans specifically targeted the U-boat building yards and aero-engine plants; in contrast 'Harris's men gutted the center of the city', to use American historian Donald Miller's words, an action that caused so much smoke that it prevented the US bombers from seeing their precise targets. For Harris, the entire city and its population was the target, whilst direct effects on specific industries were a by-product of this method, not the main intention.

Within this concept of operational practice, Harris' interpretation of the Combined Bomber Offensive (CBO) was enshrined in the instruction for Operation *Gomorrah* that was issued by HQ Bomber Command on 27 May 1943 (see Campaign Objectives). Comprising the destruction of a city in a concentrated series of attacks, it would prove the apogee of Harris' style of area bombing. The intent was fully apparent in the briefing message given by Harris to the aircrews before the second attack on 27 July, written in its characteristically belligerent way:

> The Battle of Hamburg continues. Your opening blow was first rate. It may take half a dozen for the knockout, but knockout it will be. Final and complete … In the last five months [during the Battle of the Ruhr] you have inflicted upon Germany the greatest continuous series of military disasters in history. At present that fact is only just beginning to dawn upon the exponents [the Royal Navy] of the more archaic forms of warfare. But it has dawned on Germany and resounded throughout Germany. From inflicting military disasters you are now proceeding to administer catastrophes. If you keep it up … you will have Germany on her knees before the leaves have fallen.

The *Gomorrah* raids set the benchmark of destruction by which other attacks would be judged, and Harris set out to inflict further Hamburgs on other cities, with varying degrees of success.

Astonishingly, as late as February 1945, Bufton admitted to the Assistant Chief of Air Staff (Operations), Air Vice-Marshal Thomas Williams:

> I do not think I have ever seen an official definition of 'strategic bombing'. In my opinion, strategic bombing in its purest sense implies the direct attack by bombing of an enemy country with the object of (i) enforcing its capitulation by air action alone; or (ii) reducing its capacity to wage war to such an extent that its defeat becomes practicable with the help of the other arms at our disposal. The methods by which these aims might best be achieved will depend on a variety of factors which must be carefully analysed and assessed before a bombing policy is decided upon. The objects of attack might be morale, vital but vulnerable links in the enemy's war economy, or a combination of these… To put it briefly, pure strategic bombing is the type of bombing we should adopt if we set out to defeat the enemy by bombing alone.

By this time, Hamburg had long ceased to be attacked to secure Germany's capitulation through 'air action alone', and instead was being pounded to destroy the city's oil and U-boat production, thereby lowering Germany's capacity to continue the war. In this regard, British bombing policy had gone full circle, heading back to the days of 1940 when particular industrial sites within a city were targeted. From these tentative beginnings, the bombing of Hamburg shows how the British came to develop, adopt and implement *their* method of area bombing and, in so doing, cause the destruction of one of Europe's greatest seaports. Hamburg belongs to a collection of unfortunate cities devastated by strategic bombing during World War II. Mass death and massive devastation, and the manner in which this was delivered through the apocalypse of the 'firestorm', with its fiery destruction and asphyxiation of a population, caused Hamburg to be placed alongside Dresden, Tokyo and the atomic-bombed cities of Japan to become, in John Buckley's words, 'the starkest images we have of air war'. This is the story of British attempts to bring about this 'stark image', not just by examining the bombing of summer 1943 but through describing the long air campaign against Germany's second city from May 1940 to April 1945.

CHRONOLOGY

1939

3–4 September Ten Whitleys (leaflet raids to Hamburg, Bremen and Ruhr)

1940

11–12 January Nine Wellingtons; two on Hamburg (leaflet raids)

28 March Air Chief Marshal Sir Charles Portal succeeds Air Chief Marshal Sir Edgar Ludlow-Hewitt as C-in-C Bomber Command

17–18 May, 27–28 May & 30–31 May 48, 24 and 18 Hampdens bomb oil refineries at Hamburg and Bremen each night

1–2 June, 6–7 June & 18—20 June Attacks on targets throughout Germany, including Hamburg's oil refineries

24–25 June 68 Wellingtons, 19 Hampdens and 16 Whitleys bomb oil refineries–railways throughout Germany, including those in Hamburg

30 June–1 July 82 aircraft on targets throughout Germany, including Hamburg

3 July & 5 July (day) 33 and 60 aircraft attack invasion shipping in Low Countries and Germany, including ocean liners *Europa* and *Bremen* at Hamburg

13 July New directive: Bomber Command ordered to help reduce scale of air attacks on Britain

27–28 July 24 Wellingtons and 19 Hampdens on north German ports, including Hamburg

5–6 August 85 aircraft on ports throughout Low Countries and Germany, including Hamburg

10–11 August 57 aircraft attack nine targets in Germany, including Hamburg

8 September Alert No.1; Bomber Command directed against invasion preparations

8–9 September 49 Hampdens attack Blohm & Voss shipyards in Hamburg

4 October Air Chief Marshal Sir Richard Peirse succeeds Portal as C-in-C Bomber Command

12 October & 18 October (day) One Blenheim attacks Hamburg's docks each night

Air Chief-Marshal Sir Arthur Harris, Commander-in-Chief Bomber Command (22 February 1942–15 September 1945). The picture shows Harris' determined and belligerent character, characteristics that came out in his numerous letters to Churchill and the Air Staff about bombing Germany. This made Harris unpopular with the Navy and Coastal Command. (EN-Archive)

18–19 October 28 aircraft bomb Hamburg (docks–aluminium works)

21–22 October 31 Wellingtons attack battleship *Bismarck* in Hamburg

24–25 October 113 aircraft bomb targets throughout Germany, including Hamburg

25 October Portal becomes Chief of the Air Staff (CAS)

26 October (day) 11 Blenheims attack Hamburg and Bremen

28–29 October 20 Hampdens bomb Hamburg's docks

30 October New directive: attacks on civilian morale and large industrial areas

5–6 November Ten Wellingtons bomb Hamburg (docks)

15–16 November 67 aircraft sent against Hamburg

16–17 November 131 aircraft attack four separate targets in Hamburg; hitherto largest British raid on one target

23–24 November Three Hampdens mine-laying in Elbe

1941
15 January New directive: focus on oil

10–11 February Debut by Stirlings (oil storage tanks at Rotterdam)

24–24 February Debut by Manchesters (German warships at Brest)

9 March New directive: Bomber Command ordered to assist Battle of the Atlantic

10–11 March Debut by Halifaxes (naval targets at Le Havre)

12–13 March 40 Hampdens, 25 Whitleys, 16 Wellingtons, four Manchesters and three Halifaxes bomb Blohm & Voss shipyards and other industries in Hamburg

13–14 March 53 Wellingtons, 34 Hampdens, 24 Whitleys, 21 Blenheims, five Manchesters and two Halifaxes (total 139 aircraft) attack Blohm & Voss shipyards

26–27 April 28 Hampdens and 22 Wellingtons attack Hamburg; city defences seem heavier

2–3 May 49 Wellingtons, 21 Whitleys, 19 Hampdens, three Manchesters and three Stirlings bomb Hamburg

6–7 May 50 Wellingtons, 31 Whitleys, 27 Hampdens, four Manchesters and three Stirlings attack Hamburg

8–9 May 364 aircraft on numerous German naval targets; 100 Wellingtons, 78 Hampdens, nine Manchesters and one Stirling bomb Hamburg; largest operation during this period

10–11 May 60 Wellingtons, 35 Hampdens, 23 Whitleys and one Manchester attack Blohm & Voss shipyards, Altona power station and city

11–12 May 91 Wellingtons and one Stirling bomb Hamburg

29–30 June 13 Stirlings, seven Wellingtons, six Manchesters and two Halifaxes bomb Hamburg

16–17 July 51 Wellingtons, 32 Hampdens and 24 Whitleys bomb Hamburg

25–26 July 43 Wellingtons attack Hamburg

26 July (day) Two RAF Fortresses sent to Hamburg

2–3 August 58 Wellingtons, 21 Whitleys and one Stirling bomb Hamburg's railways and marshalling yards

8–9 August 44 Wellingtons attack Hamburg's shipyards and railway marshalling yards

31 August & 2 September (day) Three Fortresses sent to Hamburg

15–16 September 169 aircraft bomb Hamburg (shipyards–railway stations)

29–30 September 93 aircraft attack Hamburg

30 September–1 October 48 Hampdens, 24 Wellingtons and ten Whitleys sent to Hamburg

26–27 October 115 aircraft bomb shipyards and city area of Hamburg

31 October–1 November 123 aircraft bomb Hamburg

9–10 November 103 aircraft sent to Hamburg

30 November–1 December Hamburg's shipyards and city area attacked by six types of aircraft – 92 Wellingtons, 48 Hampdens, 24 Whitleys, 11 Halifaxes, four Manchesters and two Stirlings – showing disparate nature of bomber force

1942
14–15 January 95 aircraft sent to Hamburg (shipyards–airframe factory)

15–16 January 96 aircraft sent to Hamburg

20 February Air Chief Marshal Sir Arthur Harris succeeds temporary commanding officer Air Vice-Marshal Sir Jack Baldwin; inherits new directive advocating bombing German towns

10–11 March Debut by Lancasters to Germany, target being Essen

8–9 April 177 Wellingtons, 41 Hampdens, 22 Stirlings, 13 Manchesters, 12 Halifaxes and seven Lancasters attack Hamburg

17–18 April 134 Wellingtons, 23 Stirlings, 11 Halifaxes and five Manchesters bomb Hamburg

29–30 April Bomber Command retires Whitleys from front-line service

3–4 May 43 Wellingtons, 20 Halifaxes, 13 Stirlings and five Hampdens sent to attack Hamburg, the centenary of the city's great fire

30–31 May 1,000-bomber raid (Operation *Millennium*); first choice Hamburg but bad weather sees switch to Cologne

25–26 June Manchesters withdrawn from operations

26–27 July 181 Wellingtons, 77 Lancasters, 73 Halifaxes, 39 Stirlings and 33 Hampdens, a total of 403 aircraft, sent to bomb Hamburg

28–29 July 256 aircraft (including OTU units) attack Hamburg

3 August (day) Ten Halifaxes dispatched to Hamburg; turned back due to lack of cloud cover

15 August Formation of Pathfinder Force

17–18 August Blenheims withdrawn from front-line service

14–15 September Hampdens withdrawn from front-line service

25 October 6 (RCAF) Group formed

9–10 November 74 Wellingtons, 72 Lancasters, 48 Halifaxes and 19 Stirlings bomb Hamburg

1943
30–31 January 135 Lancasters, seven Stirlings and six Halifaxes dispatched to Hamburg; first use of H2S navigational aid on a German target

3–4 February 84 Halifaxes, 66 Stirlings, 62 Lancasters and 51 Wellingtons bomb Hamburg

4 February Air Ministry sends Harris the so-called 'Casablanca Directive'

3–4 March 149 Lancasters, 123 Wellingtons, 83 Halifaxes and 62 Stirlings to Hamburg; attack goes badly astray (see pages 64–65)

5–6 March 'Main Offensive' against Germany begins with Battle of the Ruhr

13–14 April Six Mosquitoes on nuisance raids to Hamburg, Bremen and Wilhelmshaven

27 May HQ Bomber Command issues Order No.173 – Operation *Gomorrah* – the complete destruction of Hamburg

26–27 June, 28–29 June, 3–4 July & 5–6 July Four Mosquitoes to Hamburg each night

24–25 July Opening of Battle of Hamburg (Operation *Gomorrah*); 347 Lancasters, 246 Halifaxes, 125 Stirlings and 73 Wellingtons sent; six Wellingtons drop mines in Elbe; debut of Window countermeasure

25–26 July & 26–27 July Six Mosquitoes to Hamburg

27–28 July 353 Lancasters, 244 Halifaxes, 116 Stirlings and 74 Wellingtons sent to Hamburg (the firestorm raid)

28–29 July Four Mosquitoes to Hamburg

29–30 July 340 Lancasters, 244 Halifaxes, 119 Stirlings, 70 Wellingtons and four Mosquitoes attack Hamburg

2–3 August 329 Lancasters, 235 Halifaxes, 105 Stirlings, 66 Wellingtons and five Mosquitoes sent; Battle of Hamburg ends anti-climatically because of terrible weather

8–9 October Bomber Command uses Wellingtons against Germany for last time

5–6 November 26 Mosquitoes sent to Hamburg, Hannover and Ruhr

3 December 100 Group formed

1944
1–2 January, 11–12 March & 6–7 April 15, 20 and 35 Mosquitoes to Hamburg

14 April Eisenhower given authority over British and American strategic bomber forces; increasing focus on targets in France in preparation for Operation *Overlord*

26–27 April & 28–29 April 16 and 26 Mosquitoes to Hamburg

12–13 June Following D-Day, Bomber Command recommences attacks on Germany's oil industry

22–23 June, 20–21 July & 26–27 July 29, 26, 30 Mosquitoes to Hamburg each night

26–27 July 29, 26 and, 30 Mosquitoes to Hamburg

28–29 July 187 Halifaxes, 106 Lancasters and 14 Mosquitoes despatched to Hamburg; 494 aircraft simultaneously bomb Stuttgart

26–27 August, 29–30 August & 6–7 September 13, 53 and 32 Mosquitoes to Hamburg

15 September Strategic bomber forces released from SHAEF control

Air Vice-Marshal Sir D.C.T. Bennett, AOC 8 (PFF) Group and former Halifax pilot with 77 Squadron. In his memoirs, Bennett wrote about being 'a little shaken to find that Bomber Command also had very little 'aim' literally'. The Pathfinders were considered to be the solution to Bomber Command's problems, and despite earlier opposition Harris 'fought the bureaucrats who wanted some senior and senile stooge to command it'. The Battle of Hamburg, Bennett stated, was 'the greatest victory of the war'. (En-Archive)

23–24 September Breaching of Dortmund–Ems Canal by Tallboys dropped by 5 Group's Lancasters; repeated on 4–5 November

25 September New directive: oil and communications

26–27 September, 30 September–1 October, 12–13 October, 14–15 October, 15–16 October, 22–23 October & 31 October–1 November Forces of 6, 46, 52, 20, 44, 45 and 49 Mosquitoes to Hamburg

1 November New directive: greater focus on Germany's oil industry

11–12 November 237 Lancasters and eight Mosquitoes sent to attack oil refineries at Harburg

30 November–1 December & 11–12 December 53 and 28 Mosquitoes to Hamburg

27–28 December 'Siren Tours' (nuisance raids) by seven Mosquitoes to Hamburg, Hannover, Münster and Osnabrück

1945
16–17 January Nine Mosquitoes to Hamburg

31 January New directive: after oil and transportation, Harris instructed to place 'marginal' bombing effort on shipyards assembling prefabricated U-boats

21–22 February Major effort begins against German transportation to isolate the Ruhr from rest of Germany; supplies of coal and U-boat sections to Hamburg affected

7–8 March 234 Lancasters and seven Mosquitoes bomb Rhenania-Ossag oil refinery at Harburg

8–9 March 241 Halifaxes, 62 Lancasters and nine Mosquitoes attack Blohm & Voss shipyards in Hamburg

21–22 March 151 Lancasters and eight Mosquitoes bomb Deutsche Erdölwerke oil refinery in Hamburg

29–30 March Seven Mosquitoes sent to Rhenania-Ossag oil refinery at Harburg

30–31 March Three Mosquitoes to Hamburg

31 March (day) 361 Lancasters, 100 Halifaxes and eight Mosquitoes attack Blohm & Voss shipyards in Hamburg

2–3 April One Mosquito in nuisance raid to Hamburg

4–5 April 327 Halifaxes, 36 Lancasters and 14 Mosquitoes attack Rhenania-Ossag oil refinery at Harburg

8–9 April 263 Halifaxes, 160 Lancasters and 17 Mosquitoes bomb Hamburg

9 April (day) 57 Lancasters drop Grand Slam and Tallboy 'special bombs' on concrete U-boat pens at Finkenwärder and nearby oil storage tanks at Petroleum-Hafen

9–10 April 25 Mosquitoes to Hamburg

13–14 April 87 Mosquitoes attack Blohm & Voss shipyards in two waves; Bomber Command's last attack on long-suffering Hamburg

3 May City of Hamburg surrenders to British Army

7 May Unconditional German surrender

ATTACKER'S CAPABILITIES

'to ensure that as many bombs as possible fall on the city and in those places where it is most vulnerable to incendiary attack, the aiming mark selected frequently lies in the centre of the most densely built-up areas'

Air Vice-Marshal Norman Bottomley, Deputy Chief of the Air Staff, to Air Vice-Marshal Charles Medhurst, Vice-Chief of the Air Staff, 26 November 1942

'in the field of radar they must have the world's greatest genius … . [W]e have the nincompoops … . I hate the rogues like the plague, but in one respect I am obliged to doff my cap to them'

Reichsmarschall Hermann Göring, C-in-C Luftwaffe, 8 October 1943

Handley-Page Hampden, another of Bomber Command's aircraft flying during the early years of the war, frequently attacked Hamburg during 1940–41. (EN-Archive)

Expansion and re-equipment

On 1 November 1940, Prime Minister Winston Churchill informed Air Chief Marshal Sir Charles Portal, Chief of the Air Staff (CAS), of having 'extreme regret' that larger aerial attacks were not being made on Germany, for 'it is the rising scale of delivery of bombs which must be taken as the measure of the success of our policy'. In reply, Portal pointed out that Bomber Command was hampered by slowness in receiving replacement aircraft for those lost, with crashes in the UK accounting for six times more aircraft lost than those that were shot down. Bomber Command's strategy during the forthcoming winter, he added, was consequently dictated by 'choosing our weather and putting forth our maximum effort on good nights'. This policy of operating only in favourable weather led to a modest increase in the bomber force by spring 1941, yet fundamentally it remained too small for its disparate tasks, Air Chief Marshal Sir Richard Peirse, C-in-C Bomber Command, informed Churchill, and for mitigating 'the devastating effects' of aircraft sent to the Middle East and 'diversions' to Coastal Command. On 26 April, Air Marshal Arthur Harris, then Deputy Chief of the Air Staff (DCAS), told Portal the bombing effort remained limited because Blenheims were flying daylight operations, as were an experimental flight of Hampdens, which left just 90 Wellingtons, 50–60 Hampdens and a similar number of Whitleys. Persistent technical issues grounded the rest: the Manchesters (engines), Halifaxes (hydraulic system) and Stirlings (electrical). '[T]here is not likely to be any ponderable increase in the night effort,' Harris stated, 'until the [new] heavies are cured of their troubles and the Blenheims and the Hampden flight go back to night work.' Reliability issues persisted throughout 1941. Arriving at 106 Squadron, Wing Commander Guy Gibson described his conversation on meeting Flight Lieutenant R.J. Dunlop-MacKenzie:

MacKenzie: 'God, you're a clot.'
Gibson: 'Why?'
MacKenzie: 'These Manchesters. They're awful. The actual kite's all right, but it's the engine. They're fine when they keep running, but they don't often do so.'

Upon taking over Bomber Command, Harris recognized its destructive power was more potential than actual, owing to the force being 'very small'. On 23 February 1942, Bomber Command comprised 378 serviceable aircraft and crews, with only 69 being the newer heavy bombers. Expansion remained problematic because of upgrading from obsolete pre-war bombers to the newer heavies, which themselves were hardly trouble free. The Manchesters were withdrawn in late June 1942, which even predated the Blenheims and Whitleys finishing their front-line service.

Hampdens flew their last bombing operation on 14–15 September 1942. Moreover, whilst 1942 saw 19 new squadrons formed, 13 of these were transferred to Coastal Command or sent to the Middle East theatre. By December 1942, Harris therefore possessed only 418 bombers. A higher proportion were heavy bombers (261), however, which covered up the small increase in actual numbers because these larger aircraft meant 44 per cent more bombs were dropped in 1942 than during the previous year. By late 1942, the Command was falling short of the '50 Squadron Plan', Portal stated, largely because of 'shortcomings in the matter of aircraft supply'. Continual technical issues hardly helped. Undercarriage problems with 77 Squadron's Halifax Mk Vs saw them returned to Handley Page for modification. But probably Harris' worst trouble was with 3 Group's Stirlings, with their vulnerable undercarriage, poor ceiling and sluggish, poor-quality production. Often just 30 were available because the type's Bristol Hercules engines needed frequent changing. '[P]ractically the whole operational value of 3 Group [has] collapse[d] under us owing to the scandalous Stirling,' Harris complained on Christmas Day 1942. At least there was the Lancaster, however. Thanks to the brilliance of Avro's designer, Roy Chadwick, relatively straightforward modifications to the Manchester transformed a donkey into a thoroughbred. Arriving in winter 1941–42, even this great aircraft was not trouble free, with problems bedevilling its fuel system and sluggish production making the number available (according to Harris) 'totally inadequate to deliver the concentrated attacks necessary'. Yet its superiority in handling, speed, range, ceiling and, above all, bomb-carrying capacity – both in terms of size and versatility – really marked it out; the Lancaster Mk I and Mk III's bomb load was 9,840lb–13,280lb, compared to the the Halifax Mk II–V's 5,960lb–7,960lb and the Stirling Mk I–III's 4,788lb–5,136lb.

Marshal of the Royal Air Force Sir Hugh Trenchard, founding father of the RAF and staunch advocate of strategic bombing. His note on War Policy stated 'except by air power we, and our Allies, cannot get at our enemy in any theatre of war . . . The only force by which we are able to carry war operations into German territory and directly against the war production and industrial life of the German nation is the aircraft of our Bomber Command'. Doing otherwise meant 'play[ing] Germany's game . . . [and] revert[ing] to 1914–18' and battling the Germany Army. (Getty Images)

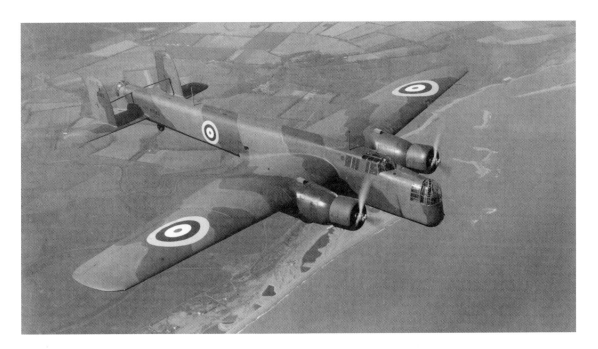

It was a testimony to Britain's aircraft industry that just seven months later, Harris sent a bomber force of 791 to attack Hamburg on 24–25 July. Greater production saw 648 operational available aircraft in February 1943 become 839 in July that year, notwithstanding the costly attrition during the Battle of the Ruhr. Lancaster numbers went from 176 to 330, Halifaxes from 134 to 243 and the sluggish Stirling from 81 to 134. Mosquito production showed only a modest rise, however, increasing by just three to 35. At the other end of the scale, the Wellington, gradually phased out from front-line squadron service, saw numbers decline from 147 in February to 97 by July. Numbers also improved because the practice of sending bombers to other commands and theatres, if not ceasing completely, had lessened by mid-1943. This, of course, greatly impacted the bomb tonnage dropped on Germany. The two Hamburg attacks of late July 1942 saw 1,051 aircraft drop 2,043 tons of bombs; in contrast, the *Gomorrah* raids (not including the last attack disrupted by bad weather) saw 2,344 bombers drop 7,196 tons of bombs.

Expansion in 1943 also included a new formation. On 1 December 1943, 100 (Bomber Support) Group was formed for deploying countermeasures in support of bombing operations under Air Vice-Marshal E.B. Addison. Packed with gadgets, 100 Group's aircraft aimed to gain the upper hand over Germany's air defences, confusing the early-warning radars and plotting system, and by making feint attacks. Twelve months later, it comprised 140 aircraft, with squadrons of Mosquitoes (seven), Halifaxes (three) and Fortresses, Liberators and Stirlings (one each). Some Mosquitoes from the Group were fitted with Mk IV AI (airborne interception) radar to carry out 'Serrate' intruder operations, which involved low-level patrolling over German airfields and shooting down night fighters as they took off.

By winter 1944–45, Bomber Command's front-line strength had become exceptionally large. In Harris' words the Command had 'reached the peak of expansion', dominated by Lancasters and modern versions of the Halifax. Although telling the Air Ministry in April 1943 that improving the Halifax Mk III was 'an inexcusable waste of manpower and materials', it had become a fine aircraft (especially the Mk VI version), whose performance was certainly much closer to the Lancaster's. With 53 Lancaster, 17 Halifax Mk III, three Halifax Mk VII and ten Mosquito squadrons, Harris could make huge attacks on one target, such as 1,108 aircraft attacking Dortmund on 12 March 1945, or on two or three

Armstrong-Whitworth Whitley, one of Bomber Command's early-war aircraft. Squadron commander, Grp-Capt. Alexander Vivian 'Tom' Sawyer, DFC, remembered this aircraft with fondness; 'sturdy aeroplane with few vices', comfortable to fly if 'a trifle on the slow side', able to take 'a lot of punishment' and well liked by operational aircrews. The Whitley was the first British aircraft to drop something on Hamburg, namely leaflets on 3–4 September 1939. Depicted is an early prototype flying in 1937. (Getty Images) targets per night, such as on 7–8 March, when 234 bombers attacked Harburg, 256 went to Hemmingstadt and 526 bombed Dessau. Coupled with numerous aircraft from 100 Group, a total of 1,276 aircraft were used. The number of Mosquitoes available to Bomber Command was also staggering by 1945, with 8 Group's Light Night Striking Force (LNSF) comprising ten squadrons and undertaking sizeable operations. Forces of 53 and 87 Mosquitoes bombed Hamburg on 30 November–1 December 1944 and 13–14 April 1945 respectively.

Technical devices and countermeasures

Electronic devices and countermeasures available to Bomber Command were, put simply, designed to either assist with navigation, allow dropping the bomb loads more accurately or help prevent attack by the Luftwaffe. In terms of navigation, the technology available between 1939 and 1941 was non-existent; navigators relied on maps, compasses, a sextant and pure hope to visually identify notable ground features. Through these means, each aircraft navigated its own way to the target. Notwithstanding the undoubted bravery of aircrews, it was hardly a recipe for success. Routing became slightly more co-ordinated during 1941 but remained a decision made at group or squadron level. Evidence nonetheless mounted of the pressing need for assisting aircrews with navigation. As early as November 1940, Peirse asked the Air Ministry to develop technical aids, yet when Harris became C-in-C 15 months later it 'still [remained] one of the main problems awaiting solution' (Harris), notwithstanding the alarming findings of the Butt Report – an investigation into the accuracy, or otherwise, of Bomber Command raids – which reflected the consequences of transitioning to night bombing when the technical equipment to do so was completely lacking.

By January 1943, the drive to improve navigational capabilities had yielded not just Gee (arriving in spring 1942) but also Oboe and H2S. Oboe, whose range was limited to 300 miles (until Oboe stations were established on the continent in summer 1944), was used by Mosquitoes for leading the destruction of the Ruhr from March–July 1943. Yet its limited range, coupled with its susceptibility to German jamming, made it necessary to introduce H2S. Though a navigation aid, tests with it found water appeared dark, land appeared

Handley-Page Halifax. Bennett wrote that 'the Halifax was not as good as the Lancaster, but nevertheless did a sound job of work, in spite of the fact that the C.-in-C. 'heartily disliked it'. Halifax aircrews were well aware of the pecking-order of the heavy-bombers, 'envious of the Lancaster crews but, at the same time, we felt superior to the Stirling crews', recalled Sgt T. Nelson of 51 Squadron. (EN-Archive)

lighter and built-up areas were distinguishable, so the TRE (Telecommunications Research Establishment) informed the Air Staff that the device 'offers the likelihood of successful target identification and accurate location', in other words a blind-bombing instrument. First used operationally against Hamburg on 30–31 January 1943, considered an easier target given its unique position on the coast and large river dissecting it, H2S sets could easily become inoperable and, as shown by the debacle against Hamburg on 3–4 March (see pages 64–65), not foolproof either. Indeed, although highly satisfactory as a navigational aid, its use for target-marking was more problematic, in which misidentification was highly likely. On 19–20 February, a new built-up area was mistaken for the centre of Wilhelmshaven, whilst H2S did not prevent severe bombing errors from occurring on the Pilsen operations in April and May 1943. Pre-*Gomorrah*, H2S's most impressive success was undoubtedly on 20–21 April, when 160 acres of Stettin was destroyed. The experimental attack on Münster on 11–12 June, carried out solely by 72 Pathfinder aircraft, was described by HQ Bomber Command as 'the preliminary to the series of attacks on Hamburg' because 8 Group had gained further experience of marking a target through using H2S.

Bomber Command's countermeasures		
Codename	Description and Purpose	Date introduced operationally
Monica	Warning device in aircraft alerting approach of hostile aircraft; abandoned in September 1944	June 1942
Boozer	Airborne warning device	November 1942
Mandrel	Air–ground system for jamming Freya early-warning radar	December 1942
Tinsel	Airborne transmitter for jamming HF–RT	December 1942
Ground Grocer	Transmitter at Dunwich jamming AI	April 1943
Window	Metallized paper for jamming early-warning radars and AI radars	July 1943
Ground Cigar	Ground transmitter jamming VHF–RT	July 1943
Airborne Cigar (ABC)	Airborne transmitter (carried solely in 101 Squadron aircraft) jamming VHF–RT	October 1943
Corona	Transmitter jamming running commentary or transmitting false messages	October 1943
Fishpond	Warning devices in aircraft showing hostile aircraft approaching	October 1943
Dartboard	High-powered transmitter jamming Stuttgart transmitter musical codes	January 1944
Drumstick	Airborne device jamming W–T transmissions	January 1944
Fidget	Ground system jamming enemy running commentaries to night fighters on M–F (and sometimes H–F) bands	June 1944
Village Inn	Backward-looking AI device assisting blind firing but proved a good tail warning device	July 1944
Jostle	Airborne jammer against controller's commentary on H–F band; carried by 214 Squadron's Fortresses	July 1944
Window (Type MB)	Evolved version of Window interfering with the SN-2 AI	July 1944
Piperack (Dinah)	Electrical jammer interfering with SN-2 AI	November 1944
Carpet	Jammers interfering with updated Würzburgs and GCI system	December 1944
Serrate Mk IV	Airborne device homing on SN-2 AI radar	January 1945

Countermeasures for bomber defence began appearing during winter 1942–43; six months later, Boozer, Mandrel and Tinsel were joined by Window, which was most associated with the bombing of Hamburg. Around since early 1942, following chance discovery that metallized leaflets ejected from aircraft in sufficient numbers considerably reduced the effectiveness of the enemy's RDF (radio direction finder) system, Harris had told the Air Staff on 31 May that 'it is generally wise when you think of a weapon first to use it first' before the enemy caught up. However, this was rejected on the grounds that there was more to lose than gain from Window's early usage. In 1943, Churchill then insisted Window could only be used after the

Using H2S on Hamburg

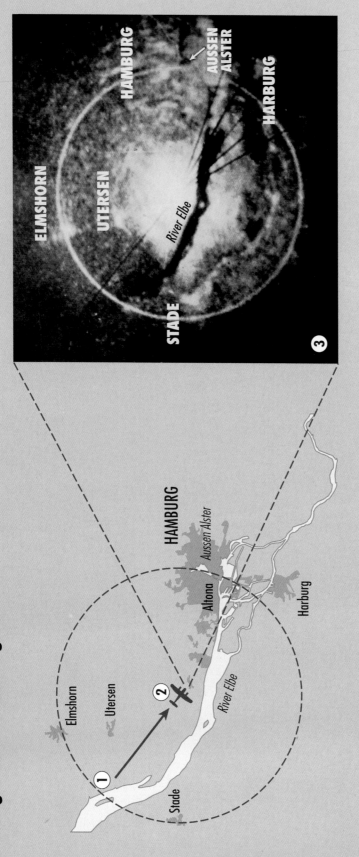

1. British bomber approaches Hamburg.
2. The bomber uses H2S to map the terrain and features being flown over.
3. The image of the aircraft's location approaching Hamburg from a W.N.W. direction is displayed on the radio-operator's H2S screen. The features of Hamburg can be seen, such as the Aussen Alster and the mass of built-up area around the Altona area, but the River Elbe is particularly distinctive. Against targets further inland, and without a major river going through it, H2S was often a frustrating device to use.

Allied landings in Sicily (he feared the Germans copying it, allowing Luftwaffe attacks on Allied-held ports in the Mediterranean). In so doing, the Prime Minister ignored calculations that Window could expect to save Bomber Command some 455 bombers and aircrews in the eight months following 15 May 1943; its use was finally sanctioned on 24 July. It took the form of a 2lb bundle of 2,200 aluminium strips measuring 25x2cm dropped every one to two minutes, each bundle took 30 seconds to split open and remained effective for between 15 and 20 minutes. An individual bomber carried between 350 and 400lb of Window, which ultimately blinded the Würzburg radars assisting flak batteries and the AI radars carried by night fighters. 'With ridiculous strips of tinfoil they could now lure the entire German Night-Fighter Arm onto false trails and reach their own target unmolested,' Luftwaffe night fighter pilot Hauptmann Wilhelm Johnen later wrote. This countermeasure fitted alongside Mandrel, which jammed the Freya early-warning radars, and Tinsel, which deployed engine noise to drown out radio communications between the ground controllers and night fighters. 'Together,' the Air Staff expected, '[they] should ensure the complete paralysis of the whole enemy GCI [ground-controlled interception] system.' Twelve aircraft (1.5 per cent) were lost on 24–25 July, which amounted to a saving of 70–80 aircraft when judged by the 6.1 per cent losses of the six previous attacks on Hamburg.

Countering night fighters was also achieved through the more aggressive approach of hunting and shooting them down. Intruder operations, using the Serrate device to detect the Lichtenstein AI radar, tentatively began by mid-1943, and Fighter Command's Beaufighters shot down several night fighters. Doing so, in Harris' words, disposed 'of some of the experts on whom they so largely depend' and 'cut short the careers of other German pilots before they have a chance of becoming experts'. He also believed it good for the morale of British aircrews knowing that the stealthy night fighter was itself being hunted, and caught. Harris therefore wanted the Serrate intruder force expanded to 100 aircraft 'to operate in support of every major Bomber Command attack', yet only from mid-1944 was it approaching that size.

By autumn 1944, the Luftwaffe's loss of the extensive early-warning radar network in northern France and Belgium meant sole reliance was placed on radars and the observer corps in Germany itself. This came at the moment when the techniques of the Mandrel screen and Window diversionary operations were being perfected, and 'these two RCM [radio countermeasures] instruments were chiefly responsible for reducing the enemy night defensive system to a state of impotence' (Harris). Bombers could now get to within 50 miles of Germany's border before being plotted, often bursting through unexpectedly from the Mandrel screen, whilst confusion reigned amongst the German controllers over what exactly were the real operations and what were feint attacks; night fighters thus either became slow in reacting or went in the wrong direction. Overall, the RCM offensive and the disintegration of German air defences in the Low Countries from September 1944, the AHB Narrative states, 'combined to deal the enemy defences a blow from which they never recovered'. After this time, 'there were no major technical innovations in RCM'; none was needed, given all German radars and signals could be jammed by countermeasures already available.

Bombing methods

The first significant change in bombing methodology happened within months of war breaking out in September 1939. A pre-war belief that high levels of accuracy could be achieved in daylight (an Air Ministry conference in 1938 stated the maximum bombing error would be 300 yards!) had continued because of doubts over the efficacy of night bombing.

Short Stirling. Though containing serious design flaws and operationally troublesome, some aircrews became fond of this large aircraft. One former 15 Squadron pilot, Flight Sergeant Thomas Charles Seymour-Cooke, recalled, 'the Stirling I liked . . . We could half roll a Stirling, believe it or not. It was very light on the ailerons because they had cut the wing down to 99ft from 102 so it would go in a hundred foot hangar. This was pre-war planning. But it had the advantage of having a very quick roll'. (Getty Images)

Bomber Command thus entered the war with fairy-tale hopes that were soon exposed by the terrible vulnerability of unescorted daylight bomber formation. Air battles on 14 and 18 December 1939 saw 34 Wellingtons shot down by Me.109s and flak guns. The main bombing effort switched to night-time, although six months elapsed before it began with the attack on Mönchengladbach on 11–12 May 1940.

Another significant development came following the Luftwaffe's infamous attack on Coventry in mid-November 1940. Thereafter, Portal asked Peirse about 'what sort of a concentration we could produce against a German town if we decided to pick our night and then go full out with everything we have'. 'The idea', the CAS explained, was 'to produce the same sort of destruction' as Coventry, beginning with a heavy incendiary attack, then continuous HEs (high explosive) and followed by more IBs (incendiary bombs). Focusing the entire bomber force on one industrial area was first tried against Mannheim on 16–17 December, and by mid-January 1941 Peirse informed Portal that concentrated attacks were 'conducive to better effect'. Moreover, Sydney Bufton – at the time serving as a wing commander – believed this method should be used repeatedly in 'delivering concentrated and continuous large-scale blitz attacks on German North Sea cities'. Aware 'recent evidence' revealed aiming errors 'considerably greater' than first thought, Bufton believed this could be partially compensated by 'attacking the same city or town at least 3–4 times on successive nights' because this 'greatly increased [the] possibilities of serious fire outbreaks due to lack of water', thus causing widespread destruction. The success of repeat attacks stemmed from the definite evidence of the Luftwaffe's attacks against Britain during winter 1940–41. By July 1941, Portal told Churchill 'our first principle' was heavy attack on primary targets, which included making repeat attacks 'to get the maximum morale and material value'. Termed the 'raid series', this method allowed insufficient time for city authorities to undertake vital repairs to damaged areas, which impacted on the civilian population. Pioneered against Münster, Aachen and Osnabrück, it soon revealed problems of food shortages, inadequate temporary housing, interrupted local transportation, increasing squalor, poor hygiene and threat of disease. Reichsmarschall Hermann Göring, head of the Luftwaffe, later told British interrogators 'nothing is more terrible than an attack which is made on the same target three times in a row. That really undermines the resistance of the people.' By mid-1943, the repeat attack had become a staple of Harris' air offensive against Germany. On 28–29 June, 3–4 July and again five nights later, Cologne was bombed, causing cumulative material and – it was hoped – morale damage.

Avro Lancaster. An impressive silhouette of this legendary aircraft being first delivered to 44 Squadron on 24 December 1941, 'a magnificent Christmas present for the squadron', was how WAAF officer, Pip Beck, remembered it. It would take some considerable time before this aircraft was completely trouble free, and available in sufficient numbers to be the backbone of the Command. On 29 October 1942, Harris told Portal that the type's excellent bombload 'has undoubtedly saved the situation, and if I could double the number of squadrons so equipped, I venture to think the bomb lift line would begin to spell victory'. (EN-Archive)

The concentrated attack, pioneered by the 1,000-bomber raid on Cologne in mid-1942, was executed not just for ensuring destructiveness but also to lessen casualties among the attacking force. Large numbers of aircraft, dropping their bomb loads in close succession, would saturate the flak and searchlight defences at the target, thus allowing greater numbers of aircraft – ten per minute (although this was higher by 1944) – to bomb unscathed, hence reducing overall losses. This meant the bomber force had to be tightly bunched, swamping the Kammhuber Line, whose GCI-controlled aircraft could only vector onto one bomber at a time whilst many others slipped through. Thus, concentration of the bomber stream was also a landmark tactical innovation, which required meticulous planning by HQ Bomber Command, a stark contrast to times when the *modus operandi* was far more casual. Squadron commander Group Captain 'Tom' Sawyer described operations in 1940 as 'rather haphazard and individualistic', with crews themselves choosing their take-off times, routes and altitudes to the target. There were other practices too. '[A] Station Commander could telephone the AOC at Group and ask if he could have his stand-down night arranged for a certain date as there was to be a mess party on that night,' Sawyer remembered, and incredibly this 'would be granted'. By mid-1942, things were very different. Squadrons had to get their 12–16 aircraft airborne at precise one-minute intervals, and assign aircraft to fly at certain altitudes, in order to allow the bomber stream to concentrate and maintain the raid's specific timings. In addition, Window was especially effective when the bomber stream was tightly bunched, allowing maximum concealment of many aircraft behind the dense clouds of aluminium foil.

De Havilland Mosquito. The impressive 'Wooden Wonder' raided Hamburg and other German cities in considerable numbers throughout 1944. The versatile aircraft would carry out target-marking, feint-attacks, photo-reconnaissance and R.C.M. sorties, and was a huge asset for Bomber Command. It became hated by the Germans for its nuisance-raiding and the difficulty in shooting one down. (Getty Images)

By mid-1943, several elements had come together to make bombing operations highly destructive, namely concentration in space by bombing one target, concentration in time to saturating the enemy air defences, and repeat attacks to achieve accumulative damage. There was also a fourth element – the use of incendiaries on a massive scale. On 14 November 1940, Churchill informed Portal that 'no effort seems too great to discover the right tactics for fire-raising'. Numerous reports and investigations on this were conducted throughout the forthcoming winter

and throughout 1941. Finally, on 25 October 1941, the Air Staff told Peirse that 30,000 incendiaries 'will ensure' that 'saturation point in fire-fighting is reached as early as possible'. Mass incendiary attack was to be trialled and 'should the result be fully satisfactory', Air Vice-Marshal Norman Bottomley, Deputy CAS, stated, 'we shall find ourselves able to undertake the systematic destruction of German towns at a much earlier date'. Following this, Peirse sent his group commanders a specific instruction (No.58) on mass incendiary attacks. Targets selected for their 'burnability' were prioritized as:

(a) Hamburg, Hannover, Cologne, Frankfurt, Düsseldorf … have closely built-up town centres which should be highly flammable. Hamburg is in a class by itself as there are four such areas …
(b) Duisburg, Magdeburg, Stettin, Bremen … have not got very compact old built-up areas as in group (a), but there are warehouses fairly well concentrated which should serve as a good target for incendiaries.
(c) Essen, Dortmund, … offer moderately good targets for incendiaries, but the chances of getting good fires going are definitely much less than in groups (a) and (b).

In preparation for such attacks, zone maps of German cities and towns were created, and when placed alongside a zone map information sheet 'show[ed] quite clearly the vulnerable areas in each town'[1] to fire, namely Zone 1 – the Inner Town. Harris inherited all this, and put it into effect with the fire-raising attack on Lübeck on 28–29 March 1942. Aerial photography convinced the Air Ministry about 'the accuracy of our predictions'[2] regarding successful incendiary attacks. Ominously, the Air Ministry observed, 'we may be able to extend our ambitions' using greater numbers of incendiaries 'to unhouse great quantities of the population living in the inner-residential zone … not only in small, vulnerable towns like Lübeck but in larger cities as well'. A breakthrough in the means of inflicting massive destruction had seemingly been found, and the Air Ministry's Directorate of Bomber Operations now endeavoured to find areas in Germany most vulnerable to fire. '[I]deal incendiary targets' were ones possessing 'a high degree of congestion' in inner city areas comprising large numbers of old, timbered buildings. Harris, however, continued to emphasize that 'the moral[e] effect of HE is vast'. '[P]eople can escape from fires', he wrote brutally, and 'what we want to do … is to bring the masonry crashing down on top of the Boche, to kill Boche, and to terrify Boche'. High-explosive bombs also gave 'the greatest service in the spreading of incendiarism' by damaging water mains and keeping firemen inside shelters. For this reason, bomb loads had to be two-thirds IB and one-third high explosives, especially as informers in Germany reported 'the havoc and the fear inflicted by the big blasters'. By mid-January 1943, maps showing the populations of Zones 1 and 2, and the relationship of those parts to the total city area, had been completed for 20 major cities; Hamburg was one of them. From a population of 1.6 million, some 629,000 (or 39 per cent) people lived in Hamburg's Zones 1 and 2, which represented 7,950 acres (12½ sq miles) or 14 per cent of the total city area. A greater percentage of people lived in these areas in Cologne (61 per cent), Essen (57 per cent) and Berlin (52 per cent). However, ascertaining the size and population densities of these inner-city areas allowed calculations on the numbers of 4lb and 30lb incendiaries required for achieving dense conflagrations in the

1   From HQ Bomber Command-HQ Groups, 22/11/41; [and attached note], undated.

2   From Bufton Papers, D.A.C. Dewdney, A.I.3c, Air Ministry-Baker, 1/05/42. (Note: in essence this is a piece of correspondence from an Intelligence body within the Directorate of Bomber operations to the then Director, Air Commodore J.W. Baker.)

two zones. Hamburg needed 1,250,000 and 156,250 respectively, Cologne 900,000 and 112,500, Essen 475,000 and 59,375, and vast Berlin 3,650,000 and 456,250, to ensure total destruction of these cities' industrial and social activity through large fires.

The final element in increasing the destructiveness of bombing attacks was the formation of the Pathfinder Force (PFF) in summer 1942, a development stemming from the Butt Report's findings and operational experience. With regards the latter, the Hamburg operation on 26–27 July 1942 had seen moonlight used for identifying the target, which, in turn, had led to a successful attack. Yet operating under bright conditions was increasingly risky; 29 aircraft failed to return, and another 29 aircraft were lost on the Düsseldorf attack five nights later, resulting from the light sky assisting the night fighters' ability to locate the bombers. The operational dilemma in mid-1942 was summed up by Guy Gibson, who wrote that 'it had to be moonlight nights or nothing' for 'dark-night raids proved nearly useless'. The Butt Report, meanwhile, pointed to the clear need for improving navigation, not just by developing technical aids but through creating a specialist force that guided the bombers to the target. In a minute titled *'Daylight Bombing' at Night*, Bufton advocated forming 'a KG100

[*Kampfgeschwader-100*, the Luftwaffe's pathfinder unit] equivalent'. Months passed before Bufton's idea came to fruition in August 1942, born in a climate of some acrimony between the Air Staff and Harris, who was against pathfinders being a separate force and instead wanting 'raid leaders' embedded in every group. Yet another investigation into Bomber Command's mediocre effectiveness (the Singleton Report) saw Portal tell Harris bluntly that 'any failure on our part to effect a radical improvement may well endanger the whole of our bombing policy'. With little choice but to adhere, thereafter Harris made determined efforts to ensure the PFF worked. Yet it would be a mistake to perceive this as rapidly facilitating dramatic improvements; its first attack on 18–19 August against Flensburg was calamitous, and operations to Saarbrücken (1–2 September), Frankfurt (24–25 August), Cologne (15–16 October) and Hamburg (9–10 November) were similarly poor.

By early 1943, however, Oboe (for Ruhr targets), H2S and the target indicator (TI) bomb meant things would improve. Marking methods became, relatively speaking, more successful and increasingly sophisticated. Whereas target marking in late-1942 involved soaking the aiming point with white flares, this soon gave way to three distinct methods. Chosen according to the weather forecast over the target, these were visual ground marking (Newhaven), blind ground marking (Parramatta) and blind sky marking (Wanganui). Using coloured target markers (reds, greens, or reds with green stars), the PFF developed the new roles of Illuminators, Primary Visual-Markers and Backers-Up. On 8 Group's shoulders lay not just navigation to the target but the locating and marking of the aiming point. Hamburg, on 30–31 January 1943, saw not only the operational debut of H2S but the fusing together of this device, coloured target indicators and the Pathfinder's new marking roles. Although not a successful performance, this was not because of what was being attempted but simply the sheer lack of H2S-equipped Pathfinder aircraft, something that would change drastically by the time of Operation *Gomorrah* six months later.

British 4ib. incendiary bombs packed into canisters ready for the gigantic bomb-bays of the Lancaster and Halifax. This proved one of Bomber Command's most lethal weapons when bombing Germany's cities, including Hamburg. 'The design of incendiary attack for the purpose of producing conflagration effects has been found attractive both in this country and in the United States', a paper by the R.E.8 department stated in 1941. (EN-Archive)

Plan of attack against Hamburg, 24–25 July 1943	
Zero-hour: 0100hrs; Period of attack: 0057–0150hrs	
Time	*Action*
0057hrs (PFF)	20 Y* aircraft to mark the target with yellow TI using H2S, then to drop sticks of flares at six-second intervals if less than 6–10ths cloud.
0058hrs (PFF)	Eight Y aircraft, acting as visual markers, to mark aiming point with red TI.
0102hrs – 0148hrs (PFF)	53 backers-up – one each minute except for four at Z+2; two at Z+6, +20, +29, +31 and +43; and none at Z+35 or +37 – to aim green TI at either (1) red TI, (2) centre of green TI (overshooting by two seconds) or (3) centre of yellow TI. Eleven crews, spread evenly throughout the bomber stream, to use H2S to check accuracy of previous TIs and re-centre attack should creep-back occur.
0102hrs – 0150hrs (Main Force)	Six waves of Main Force to bomb red TIs if visible; otherwise centre of green TIs (yellows to be ignored).
* Y-aircraft = bomber aircraft equipped with H2S.	

By 1944, multiple targets and preparation for different weather conditions meant planning became very complex indeed. On 28–29 July, for example, the Newhaven and Wanganui methods were earmarked for Stuttgart and Parramatta was selected for Hamburg.

Two important changes were sanctioned in 1944. The first was 5 Group becoming an independent force within Bomber Command, with it planning its own operations, such as the raids against Harburg's oil refineries on 11–12 November 1944. Air Vice-Marshal Ralph Cochrane could now undertake quick attacks of 15–18 minutes because his 5 Group comprised a cohesive number of squadrons utilizing their own marking techniques (such as offset marking, line bombing and sector bombing), not slowed down by what Cochrane perceived as the time-consuming methods of Bennett's Pathfinders. The second tactical development was the restarting of daylight attacks, which began following the invasion of France in June 1944 and resumed against Germany on 27 August 1944. By spring 1945, Bomber Command's daylight operations were going beyond the Ruhr, with attacks on Hamburg, in which the excellent Merlin-engined P.51 Mustang provided the escort.

The 22,000ib M.C. bomb (Grand Slam). On 9 April 1945, Bomber Command would drop this and the smaller version, the 12,000ib M.C. bomb (Tallboy), on targets in Hamburg, including a reinforced concrete U-Boat pen and an oil tank farm. The largest conventional bombs ever made, both were designed by Barnes Wallis. (IWM CH 15369)

DEFENDER'S CAPABILITIES

'There is no point in belittling the enemy fighters: they are numerous, efficient and cunning.'

Bomber Command Quarterly Review, 1942

'The Luftwaffe are a lazy bunch, nobody does any work … . The entire air force is incompetent and yellow.'

Adolf Hitler, September 1944

'You had a great ally in your aerial warfare – the Führer.'

Hermann Göring, 1 June 1945

A photograph from May 1942 showing one of the large flak guns mounted on the Hamburg North Flak Tower pointing menacingly up to the sky. Such a weapon would have been firing during Bomber Command's attack on 3–4 May, exactly 100 years since the Great Fire of Hamburg. Such anniversaries may have influenced the timing of British attacks on German cities. (EN-Archive)

Hamburg's flak defences

On 4 January 1940, a 4 Group Whitley aircrew dropped 360,000 leaflets over Hamburg and noted a few scattered searchlights, some white, others pale blue, but little else. Eighteen months later, 40 Squadron navigator John Tipton, bombing Hamburg on 29–30 September 1941, described the air defences as 'a menace', which had moreover put 17 holes into the aircraft. By winter 1942–43, they were no longer 'a menace' but a seething, violent mass of flak and searchlights. Flak defences were strengthened in 1942, with three batteries now connected to the same detection apparatus and fire-control staff, and the number of guns per battery increased (four to six for heavier artillery and 12–15 for light flak guns), as did searchlights per battery to between nine and 12. The guns and searchlights had become more powerful too; the searchlight beam had expanded by 50cm to 200cm, and large-calibre heavy flak guns – namely the 128mm and 105mm – were now used.

OPPOSITE HAMBURG: FLAK AND SEARCHLIGHT DEFENCES

Particularly well-defended, the savagery of its air defences led the city to become nicknamed 'Chopberg'. On 30–31 January 1943, many aircrews described the air defences as formidable, comprising 100 searchlights in an 8-mile arc around the city, with flak guns firing predicted and barrage form, which seemed 'like attacking a fortress'. By summer 1943, Ultra intercepts had decrypted a report to Tokyo by the Japanese Ambassador in Berlin stating that the city's defences comprised 600 anti-aircraft guns, 300 searchlights and 500 barrage balloons. On 1 May 1944, given Hamburg's vital importance for the Type XXI and Type XXIII U-boat programmes, Großadmiral Karl Dönitz, C-in-C Kriegsmarine, asked Hitler for its air defences to be reinforced, which the Führer ordered Göring to do. A month later, Hitler gave flak gun production top priority because the bombing of Germany's oil refineries had begun and these vital installations needed enhanced protection. Given its large oil refineries, Hamburg received more flak guns, although the lion's share of new AA batteries went to the 14th Flak Division covering the vital oil plants in central Germany. Nonetheless, Hamburg would always be one of the most strongly defended targets in the Reich.

Hamburg's air defences in late 1944, compared with other cities, towns and oil refineries				
Target	Heavy guns	Light guns	Searchlights	Smoke generators
Ruhr area	750	1,000	400	Not stated
Leuna–Lützkendorf (oil refinery)	475	360	Not stated	2,313
Berlin	440	400	245	Not stated
Hamburg	320	400	130	Not stated
Bremen	260	320	120	Not stated
Pölitz (oil refinery)	250	120	Not stated	800
Brüx (oil refinery)	245	150	Not stated	750
Munich	230	250	Not stated	Not stated
Zeitz (oil refinery)	168	100	Not stated	633
Hannover	154	220	120	Not stated
Leipzig	110	120	Not stated	Not stated
Stuttgart	78	125	Not stated	Not stated
Schweinfurt	44	60	50	Not stated

Hitler always favoured this type of air defence; the intense firing and impressive display of pyrotechnics was believed beneficial to civilian morale. However, vast flak defences, which in early 1944 comprised a monthly production of 30–40 heavy flak batteries, ten light flak batteries and 12 searchlight batteries, also served to denude the front lines of such weaponry and tie down huge amounts of manpower for the Reich's defence. Generally, 'the results' of the flak defences, Williamson Murray writes, 'were more visually spectacular than damaging'. Some targets were hellish for bomber-crews and MI15's plotting of heavily defended flak areas was important for deciding the bomber force's route, but balanced against this was the sheer resources consumed. One-third of the German optical industry and 50–60 per cent of the electronics industry was allocated to flak defences by 1944, at a time when the army and navy were suffering shortages of radar and communications equipment. The sheer amount of ammunition discharged by Germany's flak defences, moreover, cut severely into precious labour and raw materials needed for making other items. One study found an 88mm flak gun on average expended an eye-watering 16,000 shells before bringing down one bomber. 'Had it not been for this new front, the air front over Germany,' Albert Speer, Nazi Germany's

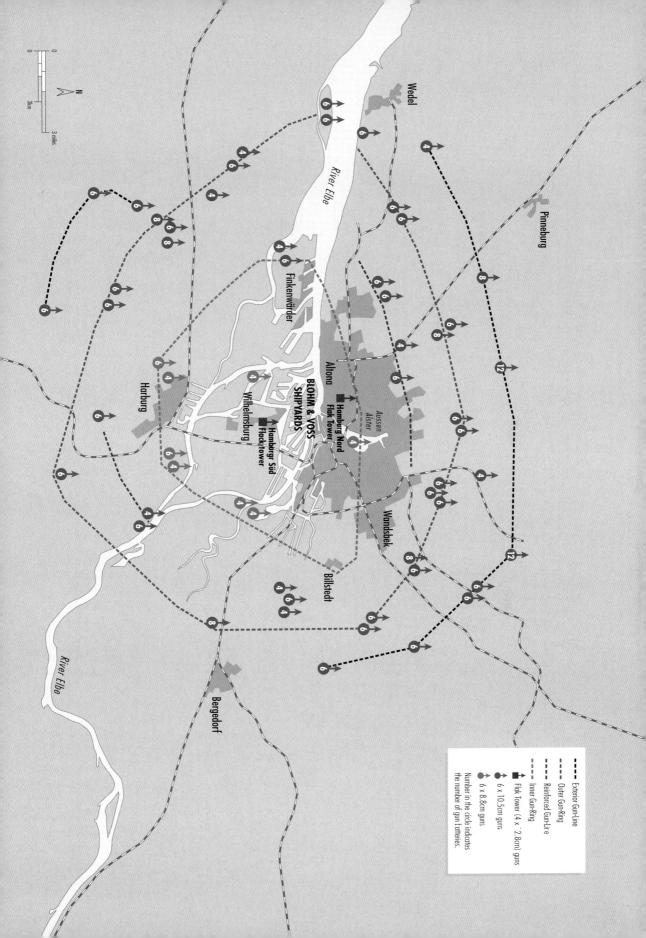

Wedel

Pinneburg

River Elbe

Finkenwärder

Harburg

Wilhelmsburg

BLOHM & VOSS
SHIPYARDS

Altona

Hamburg Nord
Flak Tower

Hamburg Süd
Flack Tower

Aussen
Alster

Wandsbek

Billstedt

River Elbe

Bergedorf

N

0
3km

0
3 miles

Flak Tower (4 x 12.8cm)
6 x 10.5cm guns
6 x 8.8cm guns
Number in the circle indicates
the number of gun batteries.

Exterior Gun-Line
Outer Gun-Ring
Reinforced Gun-Line
Inner Gun-Ring

Minister of Armaments and War Production from February 1942, wrote, 'our defensive strength against tanks would have been about doubled.' Anti-aircraft defences were organized into 11 Reich Air Districts (*Luftgaue*) reporting to the Luftwaffe's central command centre in Berlin. Hamburg was in Luftgau XI and under General major Hubert Weise.

Like Berlin and Vienna, synonymous with Hamburg's air defences were two flak towers (*Flaktürme*), bristling with heavy guns and fire-control apparatus. 'Hamburg North' (Flak Tower IV) was located at Heiligengeistfeld, having been completed in December 1942, and contained the headquarters of Flak Division 3 under General major Alwin Wolz. 'Hamburg South' (Flak Tower VI), situated in Wilhelmsburg, south of the Elbe River, was built by early July 1943. Probably conceived as gigantic air raid shelters, able to house 30,000 people, they were soon used by the Luftwaffe for mounting heavy guns on their large roofs. Armament comprised four Rheinmetall-Borsig 12.8cm heavy flak guns (firing 24 rounds per minute) and light flak guns mounted on between eight and 12 separate platforms around each tower, some 30ft below the roof. Inside the towers were chambers storing heavy flak rounds and other ammunition. These needed regular replenishment owing to large-scale expenditure; countering the US Eighth Air Force's raid on 25 October 1944, for example, saw 1,600 shells fired from one flak tower in just 40 minutes. The ostentatious size and monstrous consumption of these structures reflected the extravagance of the Nazi regime itself, but their ultimate effectiveness was questionable. A British survey team concluded the Flaktürme were nothing but 'expensive toys', costing 55 million Reichsmarks (without all the associated flak and radar equipment) and consuming huge amounts of labour and concrete to build them. The team also established the towers were sited 'too close to the centre of the defended area to attain maximum effect in defence' and were therefore unable 'to use to the full extent the long-range high-performance characteristics of the 12.8cm guns, and the complex radar'. A better position would have been on Hamburg's outer zone of air defences, yet locating them there would have meant the flak towers being too distant for fulfilling their original function, namely the sheltering of civilians.

Night fighters and the Kammhuber Line

Reichsmarschall Hermann Göring, Commander-in-Chief of the Luftwaffe, and General Hans Jeschonnek, Chief of Air Staff. Described by Hitler as 'ice cold' in a crisis, from 1943 onwards the Reichsmarschall would come under savage attack for the Luftwaffe's failure, even on numerous occasions by the Führer himself. 'Hitler treats me like a stupid boy', Göring told Luftwaffe adjutant, Nicolaus von Below. Throughout 1944–45, Goebbels' diaries frequently contained references to Göring's incompetence and need for replacement. By this time, Jeschonnek was dead. Successive bombing catastrophes at Hamburg, Peenemünde and Schweinfurt led to his suicide in August 1943. (Getty Images)

'Night action? – that will never happen!' Göring told the then Hauptmann Adolf Galland in August 1939. However, following the RAF's first attacks on Germany in mid-May 1940, the Luftwaffe's foray into night fighting began. A daylight 'destroyer' unit, ZG-1, was reassigned for night fighting training, becoming the Nacht und Versuchs Staffel (Night and Experimental Squadron) under Major Wolfgang Falck, considered the father of the night-fighter arm. Finding the twin-engined Me.110 was a better night-fighter, Falck's unit replaced a pre-war experimental formation called the Lehrgeschwader, which had been experimenting in illuminated–visual night fighting using Me.109s. A month later, Oberleutnant Werner Streib achieved the first kill, shooting down the 78 Squadron Whitley of Sergeant V.C. Monkhouse. General Josef Kammhuber, who Göring appointed on 17 July to organize the night-fighter force, renamed Falck's unit as I–NJG-1, the first group of Nachtjagdgeschwader-1 (NJG-1), which comprised 23 Bf.110s. II–NJG-1 was soon established, operating 20 Ju.88s, and Kammhuber formed the First Night Fighter Division in Holland in late 1940. Initially part of Luftflotte 2, it was reassigned to Luftwaffenbefehlshaber-Mitte (AOC-in-C Centre) in spring 1941. At this time, Cajus Bekker notes that with the entire Luftwaffe doctrinally geared to offensive action, and with victory almost in sight, defensive measures were perceived as 'a redundant fifth wheel of the war chariot'.

Generally, night fighters were found near cities frequently attacked, which included the North German ports. The tactic deployed was *Helle Nachtjagd* (light–bright night fighting), whereby searchlights assisted the German aircraft. In September 1940, however, Kammhuber, now a major-general and possessing the official title of General of Night Fighters, sanctioned tentative experiments using radar and a ground-control station to assist a night fighter to locate an enemy bomber. Results soon came. Ground-Controlled Interception (GCI) helped Oblt Ludwig Becker (4–NJG-1) shoot down a Wellington on 2–3 October, and this method – known as 'dark night fighting' (*Dunkle Nachtjagd*), developed during 1941 when radar (the 60km radius Giant Würzburg being introduced), signals and GCI capabilities improved greatly. These elements combined and transitioned into the box system that saw ground-controlled aircraft, awaiting instructions for interception, given assigned patrol zones. This system was called *Himmelbettverfahren* (controlled area fixed night fighter defence) or to the British, the Kammhuber Line. Initially, boxes were located along coastal areas so a night fighter could try a GCI first, before seeking another bomber in the searchlight-illuminated defensive barrier across western Germany.[3] Some of Bomber Command's regular targets, including Hamburg, at this time were defended by *Kombinierte Nachtjagdgebiete* (combined night fighter zones), in which flak guns, searchlights and night fighters cooperated in shooting down British aircraft. With flak limited by height, bombers illuminated above this height were left for the night fighters, and on 29–30 June 1941 Oblt Reinhold Eckardt (II–NG-1) used Hamburg's searchlights to down four bombers. The target area proved as lethal for any Luftwaffe aircrew as an RAF one, and as the Kammhuber Line developed, combined night-fighter zones would be terminated. Flak and searchlights were left to defend the cities, whilst night fighters concentrated on intercepting the bombers on their journeys to the target. Night fighting using bright illumination over the target would make a comeback in July 1943, however.

By 1943, the night-fighter arm comprised four Nachtgeschwader (NJG-1, NJG-2, NJG-3 and NJG-4), totalling 250 aircraft. Subdivided into Gruppen – for example I–NJG-1, II–NJG-1, III–NJG-1 and IV–NJG-1 – this formation was based on Dutch airfields and frequently the first encountered by Bomber Command's aircraft. NJG-1 would be joined by NJG-4 and later NJG-2, which would be stationed in the Low Countries and northern France. Hamburg's location meant bombers often flew across the North Sea towards southern Denmark, where they encountered NJG-3. By summer 1943, NJG-5 was formed to defend Berlin, whilst southern Germany was covered by NJG-6. These units were formed into the Night Fighter Division, which in January 1942 became the 1st Night Fighter Division at Deelan (Holland), the 2nd Division at Stade (near Hamburg) and the 3rd Division at Metz (France).

From the beginning, the backbone of the night-fighter units was the Me.110 because the early pilots, like Falck himself, had merely transferred from Zerstörer (destroyer) daytime units. Moreover, the Me.110 was immediately available in quantity, thus becoming the standard night fighter for want of anything else, although it was a solid enough machine for this role. Nonetheless, the story of Germany's night-fighter arm often being about improvisation now started. The drain of Me.110s to the Eastern Front during winter 1941–42 meant ever-greater number of Ju.88s were pressed into service. The C-6 version,

General Josef Kammhuber, the man behind the German air defences that consumed vast resources by 1943. Asking for even more during a meeting on 17 May saw him 'chucked out' by Hitler for 'having delusions of grandeur'. Just over two months later, Kammhuber's air-defence was rendered useless by Window. By December 1943, Kammhuber had been reassigned to the Luftwaffe's backwater of Luftflotte 5 in Norway but was recalled in 1945 to lead the Me.262's defence of the Reich. (EN-Archive)

---

3   In spring 1942, following Gauleiters' complaints about the inadequate air defences, Hitler withdrew the searchlights back to Germany to assist flak units in defending the cities.

OPPOSITE THE KAMMHUBER LINE, WINDOW AREAS AND GERMAN NIGHT-FIGHTER BASES

developed in late 1942, was an improvisation that produced Germany's best night fighter of the war. The Ju.88 may have lacked manoeuvrability compared to a Bf.110 but had enormous firepower, with the C-6 possessing three 20mm cannons and three 7.9mm machine guns in its nose. '[S]ynchronised to give a narrow cone of fire', the damage 'incurred from a short, accurately aimed salvo, and the terrible, tearing injuries that such a burst could inflict on the members of the crew', Peter Hinchcliffe writes, 'might well be imagined'. The Do.17 and Do.217 were also pressed into the night-fighting role, whilst the He.219, a high-performance reconnaissance aircraft modified for night fighting, was very promising in its capabilities but mass production of this sorely needed aircraft was never undertaken (only I–NJG-1 was operating this type in spring 1944). Although Generalfeldmarschall Erhard Milch (in charge of Luftwaffe aircraft production and supply), Galland and Speer pressed for priority to be on fighters, the Führer, fixated by retaliation, wanted bombers and vengeance weapons (the V-1 and V-2) and thus aircraft for defensive purposes remained second best.

That night fighters increasingly were using darkness to their advantage was because of technical developments that assisted Luftwaffe aircrews find British bombers. On 9–10 August 1941, Ludwig Becker used the airborne interception radar, the Lichtenstein B–C, to locate an enemy aircraft. Made by the Telefunken firm, this AI device had been around since July 1939 but development thereafter had stalled. After all, the existing Himmelbett system allowed a night fighter to be directed to some 400 yards from its target, after which visual sighting could be made. Kammhuber perceived it as an additional aid rather than providing the sole means of interception. In early 1942, selected aircraft were equipped with the modest Lichtenstein sets available, but few pilots liked it – a post-war study of the Luftwaffe called this the 'period of prejudice' against airborne radar – because its weight impacted detrimentally the aircraft's speed and handling. Becker was in fact the only night-fighter ace using AI regularly. By 1943, a revolutionary change in attitude had occurred; 95 per cent of night fighters had Lichtenstein sets installed because lighter aerials on the nose cone

Göring and Feldmarschall Erhard Milch, the Luftwaffe's Director-General of Equipment. When the Germans had captured an H2S set from a downed British bomber, Milch told Göring the sets were so big that no German aircraft could carry them, nor could the device be jammed. 'That's because they have built those 'old four-engined crates' for themselves – aircraft so big you could lay out a dance floor in them!', came the reply. 'I have never seen such nonsense in my life', Göring continued, 'The enemy can actually see through the clouds whether he is over a city or not. We cannot jam him'. This was correct, but H2S could be detected by a device called Naxos. Following *Gomorrah*, Milch insisted that fighter production had to take priority over everything else – but the problem always remained Hitler (and Göring). (EN-Archive)

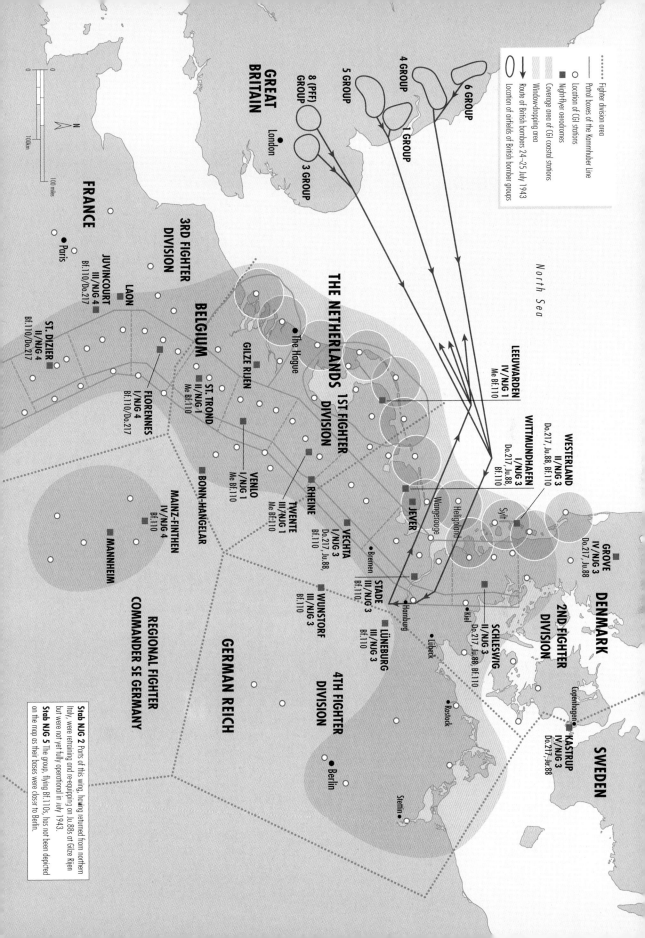

GREAT BRITAIN

London

4 GROUP
5 GROUP
6 GROUP
1 GROUP
8 (PFF) GROUP
3 GROUP

North Sea

FRANCE

Paris

3RD FIGHTER DIVISION

JUVINCOURT
III/NJG 4
Bf.110/Do.217

LAON

ST. DIZIER
II/NJG 4
Bf.110/Do.217

FLORENNES
I/NJG 4
Bf.110/Do.217

BELGIUM

ST. TROND
II/NJG 1
Me Bf.110

GILZE RIJEN

BONN-HANGELAR

VENLO
I/NJG 1
Me Bf.110

MAINZ-FINTHEN
IV/NJG 4
Bf.110

MANNHEIM

REGIONAL FIGHTER COMMANDER SE GERMANY

GERMAN REICH

The Hague

THE NETHERLANDS

1ST FIGHTER DIVISION

RHEINE

TWENTE
III/NJG 1
Me Bf.110

VECHTA
I/NJG 3
Do.217, Ju.88

WUNSTORF
III/NJG 3
Bf.110

STADE
III/NJG 3
Bf.110

LÜNEBURG
III/NJG 3
Bf.110

4TH FIGHTER DIVISION

Berlin

Stettin

LEEUWARDEN
IV/NJG 1
Me Bf.110

WITTMUNDHAFEN
I/NJG 3
Do.217, Ju.88

WESTERLAND
II/NJG 3
Do.217, Ju.88, Bf.110

JEVER
Wangerooge
Heligoland
Sylt

Bremen

Hamburg

Kiel

Lübeck

Rostock

GROVE
IV/NJG 3
Do.217, Ju.88

DENMARK

2ND FIGHTER DIVISION

SCHLESWIG
II/NJG 3
Do.217, Ju.88, Bf.110

Copenhagen

KASTRUP
IV/NJG 3
Do.217, Ju.88

SWEDEN

Stab NJG 2 Parts of this wing, having returned from northern Italy, were retraining and re-equipping on Ju.88s at Gilze Rijen but were not yet fully operational in July 1943.

Stab NJG 5 The group, flying Bf.110s, has not been depicted on the map as their bases were closer to Berlin.

Fighter division area
Patrol boxes of the Kammhuber Line
Location of CGI stations
Night-flyer aerodromes
Coverage area of CGI stations
Coverage area of CGI coastal stations
Window-dropping area
Route of British bombers 24–25 July 1943
Location of airfields of British bomber groups

Major Hajo Herrmann, the man behind the ad hoc tactics of *Wilde Sau*. Tried over Cologne on 3–4 July, it became the main tactic of the German night fighters following the immobilization of the Kammhuber Line on 24–25 July. They went into action three nights later, even though their training was not complete. 'It was very dramatic', Herrmann wrote, because this 'was the first time that these men faced this task and flew in the night without knowing where and when it would be possible to land'. (EN-Archive)

meant aircraft performance was less impaired. The tally of *Experten* (aces) quickly grew; Becker was joined by Major Günther Radusch, Hauptmann Egmont Prinz zur Lippe-Weissenfeld, Oberleutnant Helmut Lent and Oberfeldwebel Paul Gildner, who received the Knight's Cross following his 12th kill, the first for an NCO pilot. But, of course, Window then came along, in which this British countermeasure not only jammed the ground radars but the airborne Lichtenstein too. On every level, it was back to square one for the Luftwaffe night fighters.

Nonetheless, whilst Kammhuber's system had functioned it had represented a considerable nuisance to Bomber Command. Although shaken by the 1,000-bomber raid on Cologne in mid-1942, the Nazi leadership took heart from the 49 British aircraft missing on 25–26 June. Alarming bomber losses soon followed: 11.7 per cent on 28–29 July, 10.1 per cent on 27–28 August, 14.5 per cent on the following night's attack and 10.6 per cent on 16–17 September. Although 'saved' by being switched to Italy, the Hamburg operation on 9–10 November confirmed that Bomber Command's loss rates on German targets remained high, with 7.0 per cent (15 aircraft) failing to return. Greater skill and experience, growing numbers of night fighters, an expanding Himmelbett system and more Lichtenstein sets becoming available were allowing the Luftwaffe to make serious inroads into Bomber Command's squadrons.

By late 1942, the Kammhuber Line ran from the tip of Denmark to the north-east of Paris – lengthened as Bomber Command had routed to outflank these defences – and had been thickened up around the coastal areas of the Low Countries and north-west Germany. The increases were tolerated given Germany's holding or defensive posture in the air war over Western Europe, whilst the campaign in Russia was being fought. But there were limits because the manpower required for additional plotting rooms, early- warning radar sites, GCI systems and night-fighter squadrons was vast. In May 1943, Göring called Kammhuber 'a megalomaniac' who wanted 'the whole Luftwaffe' for himself. Thus, even before the 'Window crisis', Göring believed Kammhuber's vast ambitions could not be fulfilled, and evidence suggests Hitler refused the system's further expansion because of its demands on manpower and the electronics industry. As it stood, German military historian Horst Boog calculates that every night fighter airborne required 116 personnel. This was certainly an extravagant use of resources on an air defence system, which after all allowed just one night fighter to intercept one bomber in one fixed location at any one time.

In July 1943, the British deployed Window (*Düppel* to the Germans), which proved terminal for this expensive air defence system. The aluminium foil jammed the radars on which the box system and GCI so critically depended, a development the Germans themselves had forecast as possible in 1942. The Himmelbett system, on which untold effort had been expended, literally became useless overnight. On 27 August, Göring remarked how 'the entire night fighter system generated into a state of stagnation [but owing to] suggestions submitted by younger officers … this state of stagnation has been overcome'. This referred to the two methods of former bomber pilots Major 'Hajo' Herrmann and Oberst Viktor von Lossberg.

Pioneered over Cologne on 3–4 July, *Wilde Sau* (Wild Sow), the idea of Herrmann, saw 12 single-engined day fighters engage the bombers over the target. Göring, initially sceptical – describing its pilots as 'shooting madly all over the place', led by a man he also considered a megalomaniac – gave permission to experiment with this method. Cologne's flak was fixed to 17,000ft whilst Herrmann's single-seaters flew above, using illumination from searchlights and fires to locate enemy aircraft. Following this test, Herrmann estimated his unit (soon renamed Jagdgeschwader 300) would be operational by late September, but following the attack on 24–25 July, Göring ordered it into action immediately. Window thus hastened the rapid introduction of *Wilde Sau*. Flying daytime aircraft at night remained a risky business, however, and training crashes claimed a number of personnel, including the designated commander of the first Gruppe, Major Willy Gutsche. Experienced pilots were soon lost in combat too, perhaps too eager to fulfil Herrmann's instruction that 'your job is to destroy enemy bombers, and the safety of your own aircraft is secondary to that'. Expanded to three Geschwader (JG-300, JG-301 and JG-302) under 30 Jagddivision based at Döberitz (near Berlin), some 1,000 fighter aircraft would be lost during nine months of *Wilde Sau* operations. Herrmann himself was shot down by a British intruder aircraft on 4 January 1944, surviving but needing hospitalization. Increasingly ineffective, Galland recast them into a bad weather daylight unit on 1 April 1944. Nonetheless, during summer 1943, *Wilde Sau* had fulfilled its ad hoc role well enough, in spite of some very obvious weaknesses. In particular, the method caused the ditching of a night fighter's greatest asset, namely stealth in allowing the sneaking-up on a target unobserved in the darkness and getting into the position most suitable for a lethal attack. The range of single-engined aircraft, in addition, sharply limited the time a *Wilde Sau* pilot could remain in combat.

Major Wolfgang Falck, considered to be the founding father of the Luftwaffe's night-fighter arm, photographed speaking at a press conference on 20 December 1939, two days after the air battle over the Heligoland Bight. This was a momentous confrontation for both Bomber Command's future and Falck's career. (Getty Images)

Joining Herrmann's *Wilde Sau* aircraft were those adopting von Lossberg's method. Here, a pursuit aircraft called the *Fühlungshalter* (contact keeper) stalked the bomber stream, emitting a radio signal tracked by other night fighters, which then penetrated the British formation. Once there, visual means were used for freelancing around the bomber stream. This technique made Bomber Command's outbound and inbound routes to the target as dangerous as possible; moreover, it usefully employed twin-engined night fighters that had been so hobbled by Window's employment. 'By these means between two and three hundred night fighters inclusive of the Herrmann Wing could be brought to bear,' von Lossberg stated, and Göring approved this on 1 August. Thus, from the operational level, megalomaniacs, pioneers and mavericks proved just what the Luftwaffe needed to surmount the Window crisis, particularly as the senior leadership remained bedevilled by division and acrimony. However, results initially proved disappointing for von Lossberg's method when pioneered on 27–28 August, for although the contact keeper was inserted somewhere into the bomber stream, it had little idea of its precise location. Improvement came once the Germans were able to use radio to broadcast a running commentary on the bombers' location and later the new SN-2 AI radar.

Following the Reichsmarschall's conference on 25 September, a blended approach to night fighting was adopted comprising a variety of measures:

A. Two or three aircraft patrolling the old boxes of the Himmelbett system looking for initial contacts crossing the coast (by autumn, this was extended to engaging the bombers' outward journey much further out over the North Sea).

B. Night fighters not assigned a patrol area adopting the von Lossberg method and penetrating the bomber stream on its journey to the target area.

C. *Wilde Sau* fighters operating over the target.

D. Night fighters from more distant areas freelancing outside the target to attack the bombers leaving the target area.

E. Patrols in the coastal boxes of the old Kammhuber Line for catching a returning bomber and its weary crew.

Although ad hoc in nature, this deployment plan left no part of the night-fighter force not engaged in attempting to shoot down British bombers. Moreover, it soon began to reap dividends. The Mannheim operation on 5–6 September – described by Australian official historian John Herrington as 'a battle royal' between both sides – saw the Luftwaffe despatch 34 British bombers (5.6 per cent of those involved in the raid). This operation, even more than those against the always costly target of Berlin, showed the Luftwaffe's speed of recovery from Window, marking the closure of the honeymoon period for Bomber Command following its introduction. Another operation to Mannheim some weeks later resulted in 32 aircraft lost, which saw night fighters using the von Lossberg method now utilizing a running commentary after congregating around radio beacons waiting for the bomber stream's heading to be conveyed (*Zahme Sau*, or Tame Sow).

By spring 1944, the situation for Germany's night fighters – though not at their intended full strength – was better, having defeated Bomber Command during the Battle of Berlin. *Zahme Sau* had become particularly effective. Now an entire Gruppe of about 30 aircraft penetrated the bomber stream, led by an aircraft guided to it by ground controllers. This aircraft fired off flares when the British formation was found, and although a considerable help to prowling British intruder aircraft, fighter flares greatly assisted the considerable number of novices that had come to fill night-fighter units by 1944. Moreover, the Lichtenstein SN-2 AI radar greatly assisted night fighters once in the bomber stream. *Zahme Sau* remained the Luftwaffe's standard method of night fighting until the end of the war.

However, the Luftwaffe went from a position of increasing efficiency in the first half of 1944 to one of declining effectiveness in the latter part, one post-war study concludes, because of 'the cumulative effect of poor training, shortage of fuel, diversion of effort and shortage of manpower'. The bombing of refineries, coinciding with the loss of Romanian oilfields, caused a shortfall in aviation fuel that impacted significantly the Luftwaffe's training programmes. A Gruppe thus had between five and seven experienced pilots leading a swathe of beginners, a good proportion of whom would experience patchy training. Increasing fatigue, worsened by being pressed into daylight action (a fruitless waste of highly trained personnel), saw rising casualties of experienced personnel. Those who survived described their experiences of night fighting. Wilhelm Johnen recalled the fatigue, the tense waiting and 'the menace of the British' hanging 'like a sword of Damocles over the German cities'. Leutnant Wilhelm Seuss (I–NJG 4) remembered Bomber Command's aircrews as 'extraordinarily disciplined' and he possessed 'enormous respect' for them; he feared them too: 'I was cowardly, I was always afraid, and I used to tremble' when on the ground, wracked by sleepless nights. Major Josef Scholls (I–NJG-6) described the exhausting forms of combat readiness – 15 minutes, fully kitted-out inside the ready rooms, or five-minute seated readiness inside the cockpit. Scholls added that Bomber Command's deceptive measures also caused 'false takeoffs and false sorties', which were utterly frustrating outcomes for crews 'on duty every night'. '[B]lack pills' were available to assist alertness, although seldom taken. Such accounts reveal the dreadful

The Me.262 jet-fighter. 5 Group crews would encounter this during the daylight attacks on Hamburg in March and April 1945. Though few in number, the Me.262's lethal cannon would easily shred Lancaster fuselages and wings, and several were lost. (Getty Images)

strain of night-fighter operations, showing Luftwaffe personnel held similar fears and emotions about operations as their counterparts in Bomber Command.

By autumn 1944, in all theatres and at all times, the Luftwaffe was embroiled in a battle of attrition against the vast air forces of the British, Americans and Soviets, and was losing. At night, Bomber Command's sophisticated bomber-support measures were proving increasingly effective. An AI4(f) report titled 'The Failure of the G.A.F. Raid Potting System on the Night of 6–7 October' stated how 100 Group's tricks of multiple feint attacks and numerous types of RCM sorties had thrown the defenders into 'complete confusion again'. Misjudgements by the ground controllers meant just ten bombers were shot down from 769 making a double attack on Dortmund and Bremen. The 'fine art' of 'foxing' the Reich's air defences, as Portal termed it, was increasingly working. Yet Germany's air defence problems were not just down to British tactics and countermeasures, but were also a product of the Luftwaffe losing its early-warning radars in France and Belgium because of the advancing Allied armies. Incoming bomber formations were thus detected later, much closer to their targets.

The Luftwaffe did attempt a more aggressive form of night fighting through intruder patrols over England, a tactic that was almost as old as the night-fighter arm itself. Stemming from Kammhuber's belief that 'if I want to smoke out a wasps' nest I don't go for the individual insects buzzing about, but the entrance hole when they are all inside', Cajus Bekker writes, in 1941 it represented 'the best, perhaps the only, method of inflicting any serious damage on R.A.F. Bomber Command'; indeed two-thirds of the night-fighter victories made during 1940–41 were made by intruders. The Luftwaffe's intruder force expanded from 36 to 53 aircraft in spring 1941, but in October Hitler ordered its redeployment to the Mediterranean. This decision was made not just on strategic grounds but because it carried a propaganda element to it, namely that 'terror bombers' brought down over Britain did little to improve German civilian morale in contrast to them being shot down over Germany. A promising method of interfering with Bomber Command's operations, air testing and training was thus thrown away because of dubious thinking. Only in spring 1945 would intruder operations resume; on 3–4 March, 140 night fighters attacked Bomber Command's aircraft near their bases, shooting down 22. Having just received warning of intruders, 4 Group Station Commander 'Tom' Sawyer recalled:

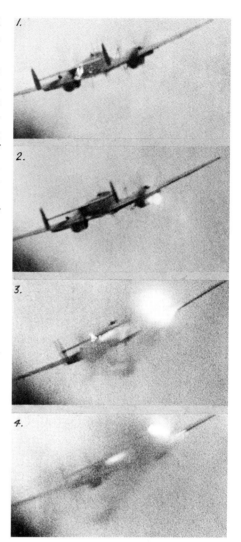

Increasingly hard pressed to counter the Anglo-American bombing raids, night-fighter crews would also fly in daylight. This dramatic sequence shows the Bf.110 of Oberfelwebel Heinz Vinke (II–NJG-2), a night-fighter ace of 54 kills, being attacked by a 198 Squadron Typhoon piloted by Flying Officer G. Hardy. Vinke would crash into the Channel, such an outcome being a colossal waste of highly-trained and skilled aircrews. (IWM C 4212 A)

[W]e saw from the control-tower the tell tale horizontal flashes of tracer cannon shells aimed at one of our bombers in the circuit only a couple of miles to the west, and at about 3,000ft. We were dismayed to see it catch fire and plummet to the ground. Our 'Red Alert' had come too late to save him, and there were no survivors. A moment later the intruder made a pass along the runway where a Halifax had just turned off to go to dispersal, then it turned to port and came straight across the hangar behind the control tower.

Calling it an 'impudent blighter', Sawyer observed the intruder aircraft climbing and dropping some 'very nasty anti-personnel fragmentation bombs [which] exploded just off the perimeter'. German aircraft returned the following night, having more success, but having lost 20 aircraft, these operations were swiftly halted. Night fighters then reverted to their pure role of defending the skies over the Reich, which by now had become an insurmountable task.

The Hamburg North (Flak Tower IV) at St Pauli, one of two built in the city, photographed in June 1997. These monstrous structures would prove difficult to demolish post-war and instead some were left, and later put to good use. Hamburg-North today serves as a live music venue and a large record store, whilst plans exist for developing a green rooftop garden. Ingenious. (Getty Images)

Striking back always extended to bombing too. The bombing of Lübeck in March 1942 resulted in the Baedeker raids being launched against English towns, including Exeter. Four months later, the RAF's Air Intelligence branch ascertained 'the G.A.F. [German Air Force] was stung into [action]' following raids on Hamburg, carrying out three concentrated attacks on Birmingham. Following *Gomorrah*, when the Führer was told the only Luftwaffe bombers available in the west had mined the Humber estuary, he exploded:

> You can't tell the German people in this situation that's mined; 50 planes have laid mines! That has no effect at all … . You can only break terror through terror! We have to have counter-attacks. Everything else is rubbish.

Hitler's demand for revenge bombing was joined by Minister of Propaganda Joseph Goebbels' public statements, writing in the *Völkischer Beobachter* on 6 August that 'there is only one reply to massed terror raids, and that is massed counter attacks'. Yet retaliation meant bomber production remained the priority. When, on 29 July, Hitler told Göring the Luftwaffe's final opportunity for redemption lay in renewed large-scale bombing of England, the Reichsmarschall quickly came around to the Führer's thinking, much to the distress of senior Luftwaffe officers. The previous day, Göring informed Milch that 'the main emphasis is to be laid on defending the Reich', yet Hitler's fury in shouting 'I want bombers, bombers, bombers! Your fighters are useless', saw the Reichsmarschall tamely agree. Programme 225 called for 600 bombers – part of Göring's 'new' Luftwaffe – for resuming the blitz against Britain. Justifying his decision, Göring told his officers: 'I can't stay on the defensive all the time. We have to attack as well, that's what matters. The British back off once they're attacked.' Under Operation *Steinbock*, London was bombed in January 1944. The following month, the operation order was recovered from a shot-down bomber from 1–K.G.2, which revealed the Isle of Dogs area was assigned the codename 'Hamburg'. Nonetheless, all this had a dire effect on the Luftwaffe's defensive capabilities, both in terms of quantity and quality. The latter was particularly shown by the tortured story of the jet-powered Me.262. Ignoring all advice, Hitler wanted it to be a fighter-bomber, but only late in the day was a final decision made on it being produced solely as a fighter, wasting much time. Bomber Command's daylight raids in 1945 against Hamburg would see cannon-fire from small numbers of Me.262s rip through the British formations.

CAMPAIGN OBJECTIVES

'[A]rea attacks on German cities and towns should be carried out with the two-fold purpose of causing death and destruction, together with the complete dislocation of industrial and social services'

'Area-Targets', paper by Air Commodore Sydney Bufton, 4 September 1941

'The enemy is today attacking our morale.'

Reich Minister of Propaganda Joseph Goebbels, *Völkischer Beobachter*, 6 August 1943

The vast and distinctive area of Hamburg's docks, divided by the river Elbe, as seen above the city centre. During the war, the port still received many tons of imports, especially Scandinavian iron ore. *Gomorrah* affected this area severely but it was back to 75% capacity by mid-September 1943. Harburg, with its oil refineries, lies at the top right of the picture (IWM C 3675A).

The destruction of Hamburg

In May 1842, Hamburg suffered a massive fire that consumed most of the medieval town. One hundred years later, the city had long been rebuilt into a modern, vast industrial powerhouse. Located some 65 miles from the Elbe's estuary into the North Sea, with distinctively shaped docks lying at its centre, Hamburg – the second largest city in Germany and 450 miles from the British Isles – was consistently targeted by Bomber Command because it was a significant cog in the economic system behind Germany's war production. Horst Boog writes: '[T]he production statistics of the *Reichsgruppe Industrie* [meant] the city took second place after Berlin, with a 3.36 per-cent share.' On the British side, the Ministry of Economic Warfare (MEW) developed the Key Point Rating (KPR) system to classify the importance of German cities to the overall war effort. Hamburg's total for its war industries, population size and population density gave it a KPR of 216, well ahead of Frankfurt on 153 but a long way behind Berlin on 545. The MEW also produced the *Bombers' Baedeker* containing every German city and town with more than 15,000 residents. War industries were ranked as the following priorities: 1+, factories vital to the German war effort; 1, major

Hitler inspects a model of the Hamburg docks, with large suspension bridge taking the autobahn over the Elbe. On Hitler's left are Dr Fritz Todt and Heinrich Himmler (nearest the camera); on his right are Karl Kaufmann and Erich Raeder. Hamburg was one of the cities Hitler planned to rebuild after the war. (Getty Images)

plants in major industries; 2, minor plants in major industries or major plants in minor industries; and 3, factories of little importance to the German war economy. Hamburg – and its satellite towns of Harburg and Wilhelmsburg – came fourth behind Berlin, Duisburg and Bochum–Gelsenkirchen because of its two shipbuilding yards and oil refinery, graded Priority 1+ targets. Numerous other targets, seen in the accompanying charts below, only added to the city's importance. Thus, Portal, the CAS, told Churchill on 24 July 1943 that Hamburg 'is much more than a dormant centre of peace-time commerce'. Rejecting radar pioneer Sir Henry Tizard's plea to Churchill two days before about sparing the city, Portal emphasized: 'I certainly do not think we should refrain from bombing [this] … very important objective [whose] destruction … would hasten the end of the war.'

Traditionally, Hamburg's reputation was built on trade and commerce, which in 1937 had a merchant fleet comprising 2.3 million tons or 1,538 ships, carrying 18 million tons of imports and exports of 7.5 million tons. These transited through the vast dock complex comprising 22 miles of quaysides, 110 miles of docks and 165 miles of waterfront, and two port areas. On the Elbe's northern side was the old harbour, around which lay the densely populated city of around 1.7 million people. This area featured the notable landmark of the Alster Lakes, which sprang from a tributary of the Elbe, and dissecting these was the Lombard Bridge, carrying one of the few road connections between the business centre of Hamburg and the Altstadt (old town), containing the head offices of shipping companies and the main retail area. The modern port was constructed between 1871 and 1914 along the Elbe's south bank and became a major centre for crude oil storage and refining in Harburg. Hamburg's major shipbuilding yards, engineering and armament firms, aircraft component factories, a chemical works and a rubber–tyre plant were situated here. Huge grain silos, produce warehouses, food-processing factories and large vegetable oil plants stretched into adjacent Wilhelmsburg. Hamburg also possessed a railway network of 138km, nine major complexes of goods stations, marshalling yards and a large tramway system. All were considered fair game in that blunt but destructive instrument of area bombing that was designed to reduce Hamburg's ability, in all ways, to produce items for Germany's war machine.

Whether these war industries affected the politics of Hamburg's population is open to question. Years later, a resident from Hannover, Lina Hornblower, was asked if that city was a left-wing one, replying that although 'the SPD [Social Democratic Party] was fairly strong', Hannover 'was [n]ever regarded as a "red" town, not in the same sense as Hamburg was'. City elections in 1931 saw the Nazis secure 26.2 per cent of the vote, just behind the SPD and ahead of the communists, hardly indicating Hamburg was a bastion of extensive support for Hitler. The city returned low support for Hitler in the November 1934 referendum, fully living up to 'its reputation as a dangerous centre of [left-wing] revolution', as Hitler biographer Ian Kershaw writes. Only once vast rearmament began, which in Hamburg's case meant warship construction in the city's shipyards – leading to greater employment and recovery from the Great Depression – would ambivalence towards Hitler somewhat subside. Yet the British perceived Hamburg's population as anti-Nazi and fundamentally pro-British. Moreover, before Operation *Gomorrah* commenced, Arthur Harris (erroneously) told his aircrews that 'Hamburg … was the place where the rot started which spread throughout Germany in [November] 1918', the notable centres of mutiny being Wilhelmshaven and Kiel. To Bomber Command, Hamburg's leftist leanings made the population seem a weak link, which exploited by bombing could become quickly demoralized and liable to turn against the regime; assessing the accuracy of this perception requires a more detailed study.

Hamburg's shipyards		
Firm	Location and distance from city centre	Priority and description
Blohm & Voss	Steinwärder, 2½ miles south-west on south bank of northern Elbe	(1): Germany's most important shipbuilding firm. Constructed all types of warship but exclusively built U-boats during the war, producing 171 Type VII-C and 50 prefabricated Type XXIs. Possessing eight slips measuring between 250ft and 926ft, seven floating docks and a 1,000ft graving dock, the 145-acre site also contained a large engineering works, making MAN diesel engines, boilers and aircraft components. Employing between 15,000 and 17,000 workers, the USSBS described Blohm & Voss as comparable to the Newport News shipyards in Virginia.
Deutsche Werft AG	Finkenwärder, 6 miles west on south bank of northern Elbe	(2): The second-largest private shipyard in Germany. Equipped with six slips 850ft long and a total width of 500ft, and one floating dock. Contained five reinforced concrete shelters protecting U-boats being fitted out.
Deutsche Werft AG	Reiherstieg, 1 mile south on north bank of northern Elbe	(2): Constructing escort vessels, minesweepers, freighters, tankers and tank landing craft, during the war it also constructed and repaired merchant ships. The yards had two slips of 330–500ft and four floating docks, and employed 3,000 workers.
Howaldtswerke AG	Ross-Hafen, 3 miles south-west beyond the south bank of northern Elbe	(2): Specializing in building large passenger vessels before the war, Howaldtswerke produced 33 Type VII-C submarines and 71 hull sections for the Type XXI U-boat. Employing some 6,000 workers on its 120-acre site, the shipyard contained four slips of 650ft with overhead gantries and camouflage cradles, four floating docks, one double and two single slips for major vessels, a reinforced concrete submarine shelter consisting of two wet pens, and workshops producing licence-built MAN diesel engines for submarines.
H.C. Stülcken & Sohn	Steinwärder, 2 miles south-west on south bank of northern Elbe	(3): Employing some 1,500 workers, the shipyard had three open slips of 300ft, camouflaged to represent flat-roofed buildings similar to those on the nearby quayside, and four floating docks. From 1940, the yard concentrated mainly on building 500-ton type submarines as well as 600-ton minesweepers.

Much more apparent was Hamburg's efficient shipyards, which made the city 'the most important shipbuilding centre in Germany'. They produced 35 per cent of Germany's U-boats (408 of 1,131 made), which was greater than any other port. Warships, most notably the *Bismarck*, and merchant ships were also built in Hamburg. During the war, Hamburg's shipyards were monitored by frequent reconnaissance flights. Photographs taken during April 1944 revealed a new model of U-boat. By October that year, the Allies worried its increasing production meant Dönitz would reopen the Battle of the Atlantic. The new model comprised the Type XXI (250ft long and weighing 1,600 tons), made at Blohm & Voss,

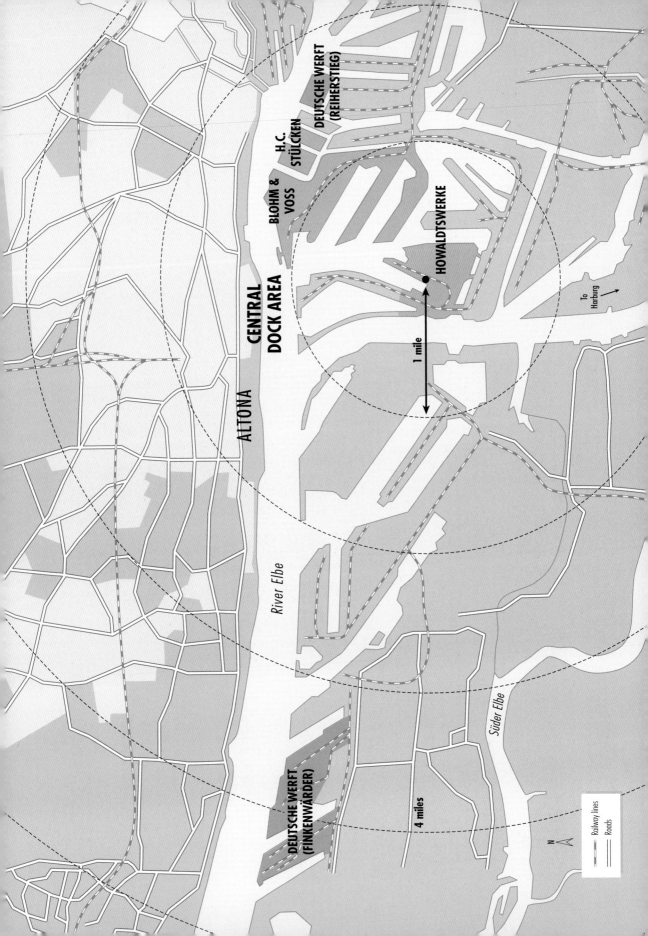

ALTONA

CENTRAL
DOCK AREA

BLOHM &
VOSS

H.C.
STÜLCKEN

DEUTSCHE WERFT
(REIHERSTIEG)

HOWALDTSWERKE

1 mile

To
Harburg

River Elbe

Süder Elbe

DEUTSCHE WERFT
(FINKENWÄRDER)

4 miles

N

Railway lines
Roads

OPPOSITE THE SHIPYARDS OF HAMBURG

and also the Type XXIII (110ft long and weighing between 190 and 250 tons), produced at Howaldtswerke. Seemingly representing a considerable technological advancement, with greatly enhanced endurance and underwater speed and quieter electric engines, prefabricated construction cut the time on assembly slips to between 11 and 19 weeks. Hull sections, eight for the Type XXI and four for the Type XXIII, had internal fittings and machinery installed, which eliminated the difficulties of working inside a closed hull, speeding up building time. By early 1945, the MEW believed the programme for Type XXIs involved producing 38 per month, but this figure would never be achieved. Prefabricated construction, whilst quicker, carried important implications. Hull sections and other components, often made in the Ruhr and needing movement by railway or canal barge, meant transportation targets became part of the air campaign designed to impede Hamburg's U-boat production.

However, protecting assembly of Type XXIs, and vessels already completed, was the concrete U-boat shelter at the Deutsche Werft shipyards at Finkenwärder, located on a peninsula along the southern bank of the Elbe. Started in March 1941, two pens were completed seven months later and three more were added in 1943–44, sheltering U-boats being fitted out, thus reducing the amount of time vessels were on vulnerable unprotected slips. Truly monstrous in size, the U-boat pens were 518ft long, 442ft in width and 26–40ft in height, built from reinforced concrete. Roof thickness ranged from 9–11½ft, with extra protection provided by large steel or concrete trusses, and exterior and interior walls measured 8–11ft thick. Targeted on two occasions in April 1945 by so-called 'special bombs', namely the Americans' rocket-assisted Disney bombs and Bomber Command's Tallboys and Grand Slams, investigation of the Finkenwärder facility by American and British military engineers was undertaken to determine the destructiveness of large conventional bombs on reinforced concrete military structures.

The other major industrial target was Hamburg's large and numerous oil refineries and storage facilities. Tentatively bombed by Bomber Command during the first oil campaign of early 1941, a Joint Intelligence Committee (JIC) assessment on 27 May 1944 emphasized 'oil has become a vital factor in German resistance'. On 7 July, the Joint Anglo-American Oil Target Committee was established to ensure both strategic air forces continued to hammer away at oil targets for the rest of the war, including the five refineries and storage facilities in Hamburg. In October, the CSTC's recommended 'future policy' was 'to complete the destruction of all major oil producers'. Believing Bomber Command held 'greater potential for destruction' than the US Eighth Air Force, Harris was given a direct order on 3 November to attack Harburg's oil refineries, and did so eight nights later. Both strategic air forces returned consistently to attack these installations in 1944 and 1945.

One of the finest warships ever built was produced in the Blohm and Voss shipyards, namely the battleship *Bismarck*, which was launched into the Elbe on St Valentine's Day 1939. (Getty Images)

Hamburg's oil refineries

Name	Location	Priority & Description
Rhenania-Ossag Mineralölwerke AG	Harburg, 1½ miles north-west of Harburg	(1): Largest and most important oil refinery in Germany, with a capacity of 550,000 tons per annum. Adjacent were large numbers of storage tanks capable of holding 272,000 tons. The Rhenania-Ossag company was owned by a subsidiary of the Royal Dutch Shell Group.
Rhenania-Ossag Mineralölwerke AG	Grasbrook, near Hamburg's central dock	(2): A complementary plant to the one at Harburg; refining capacity was 130,000 tons per annum. Adjacent storage facilities could hold 121,000 tons. Occupying a 20½-acre site bounded on three sides by harbour canals, the refinery particularly specialized in producing lubricating oils.
Europäische Tanklager & Transport AG (Eurotank)	Petroleum-Hafen, 7½ miles north-west of Harburg	(3): One of Germany's largest oil refineries, it possessed one of the few thermal cracking units in the country. Occupying a triangular-shaped site of 82 acres, 75 per cent was a tank farm that could hold 100,000 tons. Having a pre-war capacity of 400,000 tons per annum, often producing light oils, it became frequently inactive after 1939 owing to crude oil shortage. From June 1944, the cracking unit operated at the rate of 500 tons per day.
Deutsche Erdölwerke AG	Wilhelmsburg	(3): With a refining capacity of 70,000–100,000 tons per annum and containing storage tanks for 95,000 tons, the site totalled 13½ acres.
Ebano Asphaltwerke AG	Harburg, 1½ miles north-west of Harburg	(-): With a pre-war capacity of 400,000 tons per annum, before 1939 the oil refinery processed Mexican and Venezuelan crude. Later, the site was used for its storage facilities of 100,000 tons.

Hamburg's other war industries, food storage and public utilities

Industry type–public utilities	MEW priority	Products produced
Aircraft and aero-engines		
Blohm & Voss – Finkenwärder	2	Seaplanes, inc BV.238 flying boat
Klöckner Flugmotorenbau Gmbh – Moorfleth	2	BMW.601 aero engines
VDM (Vereinigte Deutsche Metallwerke) – Gröss Borstel and Altona	1, 2	Airscrew and propeller shafts
Engineering & armaments		
Theodor Zeise – Altona	3	Ship screws
Hanseatisches Kettenwerk Gmbh – Ochsenzoll	3	Shell cases
Vidal & Söhn Tempowerk – Langenhorn	3	Tank tracks and components
C. Flath – Bahrenfeld	3	Mine components
Compemotor AG – Bahrenfeld	3	Electric motors for U-boats
Heidenreich & Harbeck – Barmbeck	2	Machine tools
Chemicals & explosives		
Chemische Fabrik Dr Hugo Stoltzenberg – Eidelstedt	2	Gases for chemical warfare (produced phosgene and mustard gases 1914–18)
Norddeutsche Chemische Fabrik AG – Harburg	3	Chemicals
Rubber & tyres		
Harburger Gummiwaren-Fabrik Phoenix – Harburg	1	Lorry and aircraft tyres
Non-ferrous metal manufacture		
Norddeutsche Addinerie – Peute	1	Copper smelting
Zinnwerke Wilhelmsburg Gmbh – Wilhelmsburg	2	Zinc
Foodstuffs & storage		
F. Thörl Vereinigte Harburger Oelfabriken AG – Harburg	3	Edible fats & oils
Harburger Oelwerke Brinckmann & Mergell – Harburg	2	Edible fats & oils
Hansa-Mühle AG – Wilhelmsburg	3	Edible fats & oils
Hamburger Freihafen Lagerhaus Gesellschaft – Hamburg	2	Vast storage sheds for foodstuffs
Hamburger Getreide Lagerhaus AG – Harburg–Wilhelmsburg	3	Warehouses, flour mills & grain silos
Public utilities		
Elektrizitätswerke – Tiefstack, Neuhof, Altona	2	Main electricity power stations
Hochbahn Elektrizitätswerke – Barmbeck	3	Electricity power station
Preussen-Elektra – Gut Moor	3	Electricity switching station
Gasworks – Altona, Barmbeck, Grasbrook & Tiefstack	3	Gasworks

Population and 'de-housing'

To stop Hamburg's war industries, precise attacks were made by Bomber Command during 1940–41 and 1944–45. But the war's middle years, when Harris had greater leverage over target policy, saw area bombing target something quite different, namely the city's population, both its housing and morale. Inter-war military theorists – such as Giulio Douhet's *The Command of the Air* (1921), J.F.C. Fuller's *Reformation of War* (1923) and Basil Liddell-Hart's *Paris, or the Future of War* (1925) – emphasized bombing cities and civilian morale, 'national weak points' as they termed them, would achieve decisive victory in future great power conflicts. The RAF's bomber barons, not just Hugh Trenchard and Harris but also Portal and Peirse, believed this too. 'On taking over my appointment [as CAS],' Portal told Churchill on 29 October,

> I directed the Air Staff to examine the implications of a revised bombing policy, of which the object would be to attack more directly for the next two or three months the morale of the German people on those nights when the absence of moonlight makes the destruction of oil and aircraft industry targets somewhat difficult.

Conceived during the Luftwaffe's attacks on British cities, which had seen Churchill issue an instruction 'for plans to be prepared for retaliation in kind', following the attack on Coventry on 14–15 November the Air Ministry proposed Operation *Abigail*. This advocated concentrating the entire bomber force on one town to cause 'the greatest possible havoc in a built-up area'. Targets selected were industrial cities – Hannover, Mannheim (the eventual target on 16–17 December), Frankfurt, Duisburg, Düsseldorf and 'possibly Hamburg' – places where fire could be used on densely built-up areas and high explosives would break water mains, designed to 'impede the fire fighters'. The Air Ministry particularly wanted to select a town not raided before, precisely so 'the ARP organisation was unlikely to be in good trim'. Sanctioned initially by the War Cabinet as an 'experiment', Operation *Abigail*'s emphasis on attacking one industrial area and workers' housing and morale is considered a landmark in the development of British bombing policy.

Although 1941 saw a definite focus on naval targets and then Germany's transportation system from mid-July, figures like Lord Trenchard continued to advocate cities and morale as strategic bombing's *true* objective. So did Harris. As DCAS, he wrote to the RAF's founding father in September 1941 saying 'you are right in laying the stress you do on the importance of moral[e] effect and sustained pressure, and of keeping the syrens [*sic*] blowing and the Hun in his cold cellars', and that it remained necessary to make 'more concentrated attacks which really do damage and kill Germans'. Meanwhile, the Foreign Office (FO) reviewed the effects of 12 months' worth of British bombing of Germany, concluding that 'those raids, which were (not to put too fine

A selected audience listens fervently to Goebbels' speech at the Sportspalast, Berlin, on 18 February 1943. His declaration of '*Totaler Krieg*' meant every civilian working in the German war economy was no longer a non-combatant. (EN-Archive)

The scene at the Rhenania-Ossag oil refinery in Harburg following the Anglo-American bombing raids during November 1944, with thick oil and barrels lying in the water. Several large refineries and oil tank farms in Hamburg were consistently hit by the Allied strategic bomber forces during the last six months of the war. (IWM EA 80017)

Marshal of the Royal Air Force, Sir Charles F.A. Portal, C-in-C Bomber Command from 3 April–5 October 1940, then Chief of Air Staff (CAS) for the rest of the war. Described by Air Chief Marshal Philip Joubert de la Ferté, C-in-C Coastal Command, as 'of a retiring disposition, he [Portal] did not make friends easily, and his personality was not one to gain the affection of the rank-and-file'. De la Ferté also wrote how Bomber Command 'remained the "favourite son" in Portal's eyes', in which Harris' 'private war' devoured the lion's share of the RAF's resources. (Getty Images)

an edge on it) more or less indiscriminate, seem to have produced result[s] which are all the more gratifying'. An intercepted letter from a Mannheim resident expressed 'the horrors of this night', adding that 'if it goes on like this the people will be finished'. Although the FO described direct damage to industries as 'by no means negligible', they drew particular attention to 'indirect results' of production stoppages caused by sheltering, and workers' declining productivity from sleep loss, absenteeism, transport disruption and – rather obtusely – 'housing difficulties'. Although 'definite conclusion[s] could not yet be made', reports from neutral countries had suggested 'the moral[e] effect has been enormously increased' from bombing civilians in industrial areas.

These conclusions came about when Churchill was having doubts about Bomber Command and, worse still, its operational effort was about to enter the doldrums of winter 1941–42. On 27 September, he told Portal 'all that we have learnt since the war began shows that its [bombing's] effects, both physical and moral[e], are greatly exaggerated'. Bombing could only be 'a seriously increasing annoyance', was the prime minister's underwhelming verdict, coming after the Butt Report and soon followed by the high losses from the operation of 7–8 November against Berlin, which effectively saw the end of Peirse as C-in-C Bomber Command. Churchill imposed the so-called 'conservation order', which sharply curtailed operations against Germany throughout the winter.

Only in early 1942 would several things fall into place to get the bombing offensive moving again. A specific directive placed Germany's cities and industrial workers as the primary target, whilst an individual was appointed to lead Bomber Command, namely Sir Arthur Harris, who was completely dedicated to its fulfilment. This bombing policy was radically new territory, and throughout spring 1942 considerable investigation was made on bombing and 'de-housing' populations. Using statistics showing the effect of 1 ton of bombs on the demolition of dwellings in Hull, Lord Cherwell, Churchill's scientific adviser, calculated that the greater bomb loads of Britain's more numerous heavy bombers by mid-1943 would allow 'about one-third of the German population' in 58 towns and cities to 'be turned out of house and home'. He noted that the Hull example revealed 'having one's house demolished is most damaging to morale', only the death of a relative or friend being worse.

Evidence therefore suggested it would be possible to 'break the spirit of the [German] people', Cherwell told Churchill on 30 March. Sinclair and Portal' agreed, citing the fiery devastation inflicted on Lübeck as being 'promising' – 'we see no reason [not to believe] … that within eighteen months and with American help the degree of destruction which Lord Cherwell suggests is possible [and] can in fact be achieved'. Yet increasingly this was not just about de-housing the population but killing them as well.

Having read an Ultra decrypt stating raids on Emden and Hamburg in mid-January 1942 had killed 18 people and one inhabitant respectively, Churchill wrote: '[T]o see this meagre killing they must have good dugouts.' In reply, Portal stated 'I agree that the number of killed was disappointing', showing ruthlessness in bombing Germany was far from the sole preserve of Harris. The essential element was that raids needed to be much heavier. On 11 April, Deputy CAS Bottomley handed Portal a list of 25 German towns 'suitable for "Coventration"; by June, the MEW and Air Staff had identified 20 towns considered the best targets for a 1,000-bomber attack (Operation *Millennium*); on both occasions, Hamburg was near the top. Meanwhile, Bufton, now working in the Directorate of Bomber Operations, identified that destroying the enemy's war economy could be achieved by two 'entirely different' methods: attacking key industries or bombing cities and towns. The second method, he believed, 'reduce[d] the industrial and social activity of a selected city to zero for a period of several months at least and by the number, intensity and effectiveness of the attack … cause[d] a break in the morale of the people living in and near the selected city area'. Labelled the 'blitz attack', it involved attacking 'all classes of objectives' within a built-up area, namely: (a) houses, factories, commercial premises and warehouses; (b) civilian population; (c) electric, gas, water and transportation services; and (d) morale.

On 3 November 1942, Portal produced a large memorandum for the Chiefs of Staff (COS) containing the Air Ministry's much larger plan for 'shatter[ing] the industrial and

economy strength of Germany', thereby allowing an 'easy' invasion of Western Europe. Calling for the obliteration of 58 German cities by an Anglo-American strategic bomber force of 6,000 aircraft by late 1944, 1½ million tons of bombs were to be dropped to render three-quarters of the population homeless. 'Superimposed upon the destruction of dwellings', the CAS stated, 'there would be proportionate destruction of industrial plant, sources of power, means of transportation and public utilities', in other words the classic effects of area bombing. The emphasis, however, fundamentally remained on affecting Germany's civilian population, which was already considered engulfed by war-weariness and hunger. Substantiating this argument, Portal presented a set of grim statistics to be achieved: 25 million Germans rendered homeless, six million homes destroyed, 60 million incidents of bomb damage to other houses, 900,000 killed and 1 million seriously injured. This was the essence of 'de-housing'; in contrast, Portal played down breaking civilian morale because it remained 'difficult to estimate the moral[e]consequences of a scale of bombardment which would far transcend anything within human experience', but conceded that 'against a background of growing casualties, increasing privations and dying hopes it would be profound indeed'. This famous memorandum represented the end of a two-year process in which the Air Ministry had examined how Bomber Command was actually to go about conducting strategic bombing.

The targeting of Germany's industrial workers and war industries was formalized in the Casablanca Directive of February 1943. Whilst US Eighth Air Force commander General Ira Eaker stuck to precision bombing of key industrial targets, Harris remained fixated on destroying the 58 cities outlined in Portal's earlier memorandum, often deploying statistics to show both success and the overriding aim. Prior to restarting the Battle of Berlin in late November 1943, HQ Bomber Command's Digest stated 2 million houses, equating to a quarter of the top 38 industrial cities and 'whose combined population is about 18,000,000', had been destroyed, most of them since March 1943 when the main offensive against Germany had begun. 'To put it differently', it continued, '32½ miles of German houses have been destroyed, 29 of them in the last 10 months', which was comparable to 75 per cent destruction to residential areas in Birmingham, Bradford, Bristol, Edinburgh, Glasgow, Hull, Liverpool, Leeds, Manchester and Sheffield. Germany's damage included the 7 square miles of central Hamburg burnt down in summer 1943 – 'a different scale from anything which Germany, let alone this country, has ever experienced', the Digest frankly admitted: with 'an exceptionally' high population density of 200 people per acre, the highest of any German city, calculations had ascertained 500,000 people had lost their homes. No mention was made about mass deaths; the notion of mass 'de-housing' implied enough.

Hitler greets workers at the Blohm & Voss shipyards. Like many industrial workers throughout German cities, Hamburg's shipyard workers were brave, tough and a consistent target for the bombers of RAF Bomber Command. The *Gomorrah* raids caused many to leave the city, but most would return. (Getty Images)

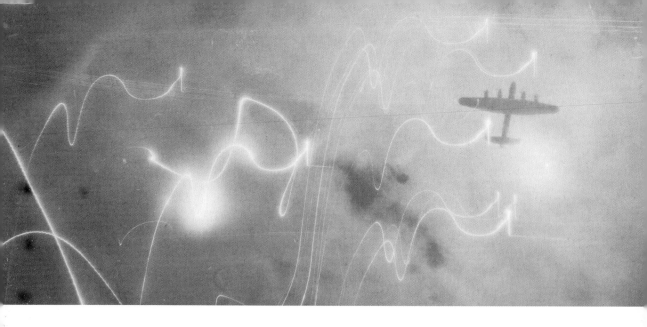

THE CAMPAIGN

'We had started the war morally opposed to the bombing of civilian populations, and now we were pursuing it on a horrifying scale.'

R.V. Jones, *Most Secret War*

Oil refineries, *Bismarck* and attacking the city, May 1940–February 1941

Within hours of Chamberlain announcing Britain's declaration of war on Germany, ten Whitleys took off for operations against Germany. What they carried were not bombs but leaflets, part of a propaganda effort to convince the German people about the error of Hitler's ambitions. Known by the codename of *Nickeling*, leaflet raids particularly targeted well-populated areas to emphasize to the Germans their vulnerability to aircraft and bombing. Leaflet operations against Hamburg continued throughout winter 1939–40, with another million being dropped, during what became known as the Phoney War, with both sides reticent about undertaking more offensive operations. This period of inaction was shattered on 10 May 1940 by the Wehrmacht's invasion of France and the Low Countries, whereupon Bomber Command commenced serious operations against Germany.

On 17–18 May, they went to Hamburg armed with something considerably more powerful than leaflets, releasing mines into the Elbe and high-explosive bombs on the city, particularly on Harburg's oil refineries. Forty-eight Hampdens dropped 47 500lb bombs, 44 250lb bombs and 15 packs of incendiaries, causing fires and explosions. Civilian Carl-Ulrich Peter Dirks remembered people flocking to see damage around the main railway station, in which a six-storeyed house had a bomb go right through it to the ground floor, destroying the shop there selling furniture. Hamburg's first air raid victims perished on that night, with 34 dead along with 72 injured, and the city remained a target for Bomber Command throughout the

Wellingtons from 149 Squadron prepare to depart to bomb Hamburg on 10–11 May 1941. The raid would cause damage in the city centre, particularly to the Kösters department store and Hamburg's Stock Exchange (Getty Images)

month because of its oil refineries that supplied fuel for the Wehrmacht's advance into France. At this time, the city's air defences relied considerably on barrage balloons for preventing low-level attacks on precise targets, but they failed to deter 20 Hampdens from attacking at 2,000–3,000ft the Europäische-Tanklager, Ebano-Asphaltwerke and Rhenania-Ossag refineries on 27–28 May. Bomber Command attacked these oil targets in Hamburg seven times over the forthcoming month. Aircrews often expressed glowing accounts over the results achieved, but these attacks were too small for significant disruption to be caused. Despite an inherent vulnerability to fire, oil refineries were not easy installations to knock out; only the powerful attacks of 1944–45 would achieve this.

Following France's capitulation, bombing Hamburg was undertaken for an alternative reason. With Britain now in peril, the Air Ministry sent a directive on 4 July 1940 stating that the main bombing effort should be on ports and shipping concentrations connected to a possible invasion. Alongside shipping at Kiel, the Wilhelmshaven naval base, the docks at Bremen and the port of Rotterdam, the battleship *Bismarck* – under construction at the Blohm & Voss shipyards in Hamburg – was to be attacked. Hitherto, the War Cabinet decreed no attacks were to be made on German capital ships because of 'the possibility of retaliation on our ships' which were being built, particularly the King George V-class battleships under construction in Tyneside and at Birkenhead. This restriction was now ruled invalid, and from 4–5 July attacks would be attempted, although no hits were scored on *Bismarck*. Focus on naval and shipping targets ended on 13 July, however, when the Air Ministry informed HQ Bomber Command to focus temporarily on objectives that 'will reduce the scale of air attack on this country', namely aircraft factories producing bombers and fighters for the Luftwaffe's growing air offensive against Britain. The alteration became a permanent change on 24 July when Douglas informed Portal, then C-in-C Bomber Command, that German Air Force and oil production targets were now priorities. Only in paragraph 10 were anti-invasion targets mentioned, namely the large passenger liners *Bremen* (51,731 tons) and *Europa* (49,746 tons), which photographs on 21 July had revealed were undergoing 'the process of being camouflaged' in Hamburg's shipyards. Portal was instructed to attack these ships because of their capacity for ferrying large numbers of troops. Nevertheless, attacks on Hamburg remained focused on oil plants. On 27–28 July, 24 Wellingtons from 3 Group and seven Hampdens from 5 Group attacked three such targets, after which burning oil was seen seeping into the city's sewage system.

A particularly vivid description of attacking an oil refinery in Hamburg comes from Guy Gibson, then flying Hampdens with 83 Squadron. Instructed to locate the target by using reflections from the Elbe to ascertain ground detail, indicating just how low they were expected to fly, the laissez-faire and lone maverick approach towards operations at this time saw the briefing officer tell Gibson and other aircrews: 'You can fly to the target whichever route you wish and bomb at any time between 1200 hours and 0400 hours.' 'Such was the plan', Gibson wrote, whose own departure time was dictated by the film screening in a Lincoln cinema. Over Hamburg, searchlights moved around madly and light flak whistled by, which Gibson banked to avoid. But 'poor old Robbo of B-Flight [Flight Sergeant P.L. Roberts] was not banking at all', he recalled, but was hit and going 'down like a blazing fire-cracker'. Intending to make a dive-bombing attack from 6,000ft before levelling out at 2,000ft, despite worrying the Hampden's feeble nose section might collapse under the strain, Gibson's memoirs read like a *Boys' Own* adventure. Levelling out from the dive, his aircraft was fixed by the searchlights and intense flak exploded all around. '[T]wo thousand feet over the centre of Hamburg is not a healthy place,' he wrote dryly, before going lower to allow his air gunner to shoot out the blinding searchlights. In doing so, his Hampden hit a barrage balloon's steel cable and flak had damaged its rudders. The evening culminated with a gunfire duel with flak ships along the German coast, before England was reached in time for early-morning bacon and eggs.

Despite Gibson's antics, concern over the surface ships of the Kriegsmarine remained. For reasons of global naval strategy, Churchill told Sinclair and Portal:

> Japanese hostility makes it all the more important that the German capital ships should be put out of action … *Scharnhorst* and *Gneisenau*, both in floating docks at Kiel, the *Bismarck* at Hamburg, and the *Tirpitz* at Wilhelmshaven, are all targets of supreme importance. Even a few months' delay in *Bismarck* will affect the whole balance of sea power to a serious degree.

Consequently, Portal attacked the mighty battleship at the Blohm & Voss shipyard on three occasions during August 1940, and twice the following month. The 'Weekly Résumé of War Operations', produced for the War Cabinet, stated that *Bismarck* was 'seriously damaged' during the attack on 8–9 September, but this was entirely false. The highest-ranking officer to survive the *Bismarck*'s sinking in May 1941, Baron Burkard Freiherr von Müllenheim-Rechberg, wrote that 'not very heavy' British attacks in summer 1940 had little effect on the ship and its crew.

On 21 September 1940, a further review of bombing policy placed anti-invasion targets above the German aircraft industry, communications, oil and Berlin. Also introduced was a new category, the submarine-building industry, because U-boat activity had now assumed 'serious proportions' and the Naval Staff believed bombing building yards offered 'the best chance of success in this offensive', with Hamburg's attacked 'when suitable opportunities occur'. Yet the focus on bombing *Bismarck* remained. Imposing just several months' delay on its completion was believed vital to assist a thinly spread Royal Navy. On 13 October, Churchill told the COS that to allow the despatch of HMS *King George V* to face the Italian battle fleet in the Mediterranean, 'the greatest prize open to Bomber Command is the disabling of *Bismarck* and *Tirpitz*'. Britain's capital ship weakness caused Churchill to push alternative ways for attacking Axis naval power whilst buying time until four of the King George V-class battleships were expected to be available in late 1941.

Attacking Kiel hoping to damage the *Gneisenau*, *Scharnhorst* and *Lützow*, the *Bismarck* – now having left Hamburg – was located and attacked by 19 Hampdens (18–19 October), 15 Wellingtons (20–21 October) and 23 Wellingtons the following night, all ineffectually. Despite his colourful prose, Gibson was under no illusion about 5 Group's dive-bombing efforts against the *Bismarck*, which 'were never much good'; 'it was lucky if we ever put one within half a mile of the dock she was lying in'. The future hero of the Dambusters raid also described being 'scared stiff' at the prospect of 'one of those lonely dawn missions to Hamburg to do a bit of dive-bombing'. Published in wartime, Gibson's book *Enemy Coast Ahead* is candid about the mental strain and nightmares he suffered from operational flying.

Photographic reconnaissance on 29 October revealed *Bismarck* and *Prinz Eugen* had left for sea trials in the Baltic. For the remainder of 1940, Bomber Command continued its effort against Hamburg, targeting its shipyards, power stations, oil refineries and an aircraft

factory with small numbers of Wellingtons and Whitleys. One attack on 28–29 October saw 'explosions' with 'large blue flashes' develop into a fire seen from 40 miles away, which was probably a gas holder going up. Following 17 Hampdens dropping 13 tons of HE bombs on the oil refinery at Wilhelmsburg on 14–15 November, which left three storage tanks blazing for two days, a neutral observer told the British 600 houses in the harbour area had been destroyed. Sixty-seven aircraft aimed at specific targets in Hamburg the following night, with the archives department and design offices at Blohm & Voss destroyed, a torpedo boat in the fitting-out basin sunk, two destroyers nearing completion severely damaged and a warehouse storing fats and lubricating oil gutted. The 16–17 November operation was a multi-group effort, each selecting their own targets in the city:

2 Group: oil refinery (Wilhelmsburg), railway goods yard (Wilhelmsburg), Edible Oil and Fats factory (Harburg-Wilhelmsburg) and power station (Altona).

3 Group: industrial area and railway facilities (Billwerder and Moorfleth).

4 Group: Blohm & Voss shipyards.

5 Group: power station (Altona), industrial area (Veddel), gasworks (Barmbek), oil refinery (Grasbrook) and dropping mines in the Elbe.

Totalling 130 aircraft, large by 1940 standards, the attack was hindered by the elements. Icing prevented 68 bombers from attacking their assigned targets; for the remainder, just a few hits were inflicted on the city. Poor weather, in the form of mist and ground haze, spoilt 5 Group's mining of the Elbe estuary on 23–24 November, and thick cloud obscured the multi-group effort against Hamburg the following night.

Meanwhile, on 4 October, following his first-hand experience leading Bomber Command, Portal became the CAS. This appointment, notes the AHB's post-war study, 'brought a more realistic outlook' to the Air Ministry and 'the reason for the initiation of area bombing and the selection of industrial centres instead of factories'. Portal soon recommended heavy attacks on large built-up areas because 'this would probably ensure the destruction of the target selected, e.g. a power station or gasworks', with secondary effects to houses and water mains that, in a catch-all effect, was believed would lower civilian morale. The policy of area bombing, so often associated exclusively with Sir Arthur Harris, was enshrined in the directive of 30 October 1940, which the

War Cabinet had sanctioned earlier that day. Luftwaffe attacks on Coventry, Southampton and Bristol saw Bomber Command respond with Operation *Abigail* against Mannheim on 16–17 December, in what the AHB described as a 'blitz' reprisal attack' intended 'to cause maximum destruction to a [single] town, with no specific targets therein laid down'. On 30 December, Portal told Churchill that recent Luftwaffe attacks on 'industrial centres' saw 'fire-raising' play a major part. Leading crews used incendiaries for guiding 'the main body of the attack' to the target, when huge quantities of IBs were dropped 'to produce conflagrations so widespread and so numerous as to defeat the fire-fighting services'. The British were duly taking note of how the enemy conducted its bombing operations. On 4 January 1941, Portal informed Churchill about repeating Operation *Abigail* 'on another town', namely Bremen, but weather forestalled this. On 4–5 January, Peirse attacked Hamburg, which like other German cities had just been assigned a fish-based codename (*Dace*). Unless this was an operation of the '*Abigail* variety', he told Portal beforehand, the intention was to put half the bomb loads on the city centre and the remainder on industrial targets and power stations. 'Overs and shorts from these,' Peirse wrote, '[will] mostly find their mark in built-up areas.' In the end, poor weather limited the operation to 24 Blenheims from 2 Group. This was Bomber Command's last raid on Hamburg for over two months, as other targets took precedence.

Targets of the Battle of the Atlantic Directive, 9 March 1941 (* = added on 18 March)	
Place	Description
Kiel	Germania Werft
	Deutsche Werke
	Howaldtswerke
Bremen	Deschimag
	Focke-Wulf factory
Vegesack	Vulcan Werke
Hamburg	Blohm & Voss
	Howaldtswerke
Augsburg	Diesel engine factory
Mannheim	Diesel engine factory
Cologne*	Submarine battery and accumulator works
	Diesel engine factory
Hagen*	Submarine battery and accumulator works
Stuttgart*	Diesel engine factory
	Bosch ignition factories
Dessau	Ju.88 Factory
Lorient	Submarine base
St Nazaire	Submarine base
Bordeaux	Submarine base
Bordeaux-Merignac	Focke-Wulf aerodrome
Stavanger	Focke-Wulf aerodrome

However, Churchill – concerned by merchant shipping losses totalling 350,000 tons in February alone – issued a direct order on 9 March for all naval and air forces to assist in breaking the German blockade of the British Isles. Bomber Command, in Churchill's words, had to 'take the offensive against the U-boat and the Focke-Wulf wherever we can and whenever we can. The U-boat at sea must be hunted, the U-boat in the building yard or in dock must be bombed.' The order was known as the Battle of the Atlantic Directive. Reconnaissance photographs of Germany's major ports had shown 118 submarines under construction. Few senior airmen liked this role supporting the war at sea. In a letter to Peirse, the CAS predicted 'a very high proportion of bomber effort will inevitably be required to pull the Admiralty out of the mess they have got into'. Such complaints overlooked one crucial fact, however. As the admirals never tired of pointing out, the war at sea directly impinged on Bomber Command because of the movement of its aircrew undergoing training overseas and the import of aviation fuel for its aircraft. Thus, in reality, Bomber Command had little choice but to comply in defeating the U-boat.

Assisting the Battle of the Atlantic during 1941

Assisting the Battle of the Atlantic, Peirse's command made 4,468 sorties and dropped 5,822 tons of bombs against many targets, and laid 154 mines. Beginning with Hamburg, mixed forces of Wellingtons, Whitleys and Hampdens were sent on 12–13 and 13–14 March, comprising 88 and 108 aircraft respectively. Naval targets were the intention, and some direct hits landed on the Blohm & Voss and Stülcken shipyards, the latter being forced to close for two weeks. But other things were hit too. Dockside warehouses, railways and blocks of flats in St Pauli and a power station (causing an electricity reduction lasting several weeks) were struck, and incendiaries burned through the top floors of the Dresdner Bank. The local newspaper, *Hamburger Fremdenblatt*, listed 57 people killed. However, what worried Peirse was the rising cost of making consecutive attacks. Losing none on the first raid, six were lost the following night. 'I shall in the future be well-advised to switch my attacks fairly widely so as to keep the enemy guessing and prevent him from concentrating his defence,' he informed Portal, suggesting obsessive targeting of Hamburg – and Germany's other shipbuilding centres – was already perceived as likely to become increasingly expensive. Hamburg would not be attacked for another month, partly for this tactical reasoning and partly because aerial photographs of Brest revealed the Atlantic surface-raiders *Scharnhorst*, *Gneisenau* and *Admiral Hipper* were docked there, and these became an immediate priority until Peirse protested at the wasted effort being made. On 17 April, Portal issued instructions for Bomber Command to refocus its effort back onto bombing naval targets in Germany. Hamburg was attacked by 44 aircraft ten days later, which dropped over 41 tons of bombs, including one 4,000lb and three 1,900lb bombs, the bursts being described as 'particularly violent', with the heavier bomb causing 'a red-glow ½ mile in diameter'.

Early May witnessed a particular onslaught against Hamburg, with five attacks in nine nights. Enduring losses of 14 aircraft, notwithstanding Peirse's concern over repeated attacks against the same target, a total of 480 aircraft (the figure for the number despatched was 27% at 609 aircraft) had released almost 607 tons, ostensibly directed at the shipyards but in reality falling in many locations throughout the city. '[N]early every part of the city has suffered … [and] is said to present a tragic picture,' the War Cabinet's Weekly Résumé of Operations noted, with the final raid causing fires in Altona and 5,000 dwellings

10 Squadron Whitleys bombing Hamburg, 12–13 March 1941

On 12–13 March 1941, 88 aircraft attacked Hamburg, which, together with another 86 aircraft bombing Bremen, marked the first attacks on cities containing the major submarine building yards under Churchill's Battle of the Atlantic Directive. Depicted in this illustration are two Whitley Vs from 10 Squadron flying between 11–11,500ft over the city, with its distinctive landmark of the river Elbe seen in clear weather. On the right is the aircraft of Pilot Officer Kenna Humby's aircraft, whilst the other Whitley was flown by Squadron-Leader Tom Sawyer. Humby's aircraft was coned by searchlights and pulled the flak fire on to it for 12 minutes. Dropping the bomb load near the railway station in Altona, despite undertaking near-continuous twisting evasive action, the Whitley suffered many hits, including its wing fuel tanks, but still got back to the UK. Humby's ordeal allowed Sawyer to sneak through the city's searchlights and flak to bomb the Blohm and Voss shipyards located on the Elbe's south bank. In the skies over Germany, one aircraft's difficulties with the air defences was often another crew's opportunity to cross the target area unscathed.

Göring congratulates flak gunners on their defence of Hamburg, probably during his visit to the city on 6 August 1943. None seems particularly impressed by the Reichsmarschall. In Hamburg, informers heard much criticism of the Reichsmarschall and some people accosted him with mocking shouts of 'Herr Meier', a reference to his earlier boast about no enemy bomber ever attacking the Ruhr. (Getty Images)

destroyed or damaged. An informant told the British 'the German people are impressed with the recent scale and weight of RAF attacks', and rumours flew about 'the terrific effect of the latest British bombs [the 4,000lb]'. The population was said to be becoming nervous, hungry and sleep-deprived. This intense focus on Hamburg copied the Luftwaffe's equally intense concentration on Liverpool (seven consecutive nights during the first week of the month). But the tonnage dropped by Bomber Command, which had further to travel, was inferior to the Luftwaffe's 860 tons of HE bombs and 13,000 IBs. Bomber Command's concentration on Hamburg may also have been due to intelligence indicating Germany's scarcity of merchant shipping for carrying raw materials across the Baltic and resupplies over the Mediterranean for the Afrika Korps. Considered by the COS on 3 May, they agreed this shortage represented a German vulnerability, and the Deutsche Werft shipyards at Reiherstieg, which specialized in merchant ship production and repair, was one of the assigned targets during the May raids.

Not attacked again until 29–30 June, at a time when Peirse was undertaking an intense effort against Bremen and Kiel, the worrying development was the bomber losses endured. From 28 aircraft despatched, the four Stirlings and two Wellingtons represented a missing rate of 21.4 per cent. Two days before, an operation to Bremen saw 14 aircraft lost from 108 despatched (13 per cent), which included 31 per cent of the Whitleys involved, which was Bomber Command's worst night hitherto. These rising casualties were the product, to quote Denis Richards, of 'a disturbing new development – German night fighters operating in some numbers'. Yet the Luftwaffe's growing success went beyond mere quantity; German pilots had become more skilled. *Experten* – Oberleutnant Helmut Lent, Oberfeldwebel Rudolph Schönert, Oberleutnant Ludwig Becker, Oberfeldwebel Paul Gildner, Leutnant Ekart-Wilhelm von Bönin, Unteroffizier Walter Geislinger and Oberleutnant Walter Barte – were making their mark.

On 9 July, following three months of assisting the Battle of the Atlantic, and with reduced merchant ship losses (July witnessed a decline to 120,000 tons sunk), Bomber Command was switched to undertaking another supporting role, namely attacking German's inland transportation that was believed to be under severe strain from the demands of fighting in Russia. The new directive left scope for attacking industrial cities and workers' housing and morale, so what had been considered an added extra of bombing now became a considerable part of British bombing policy. Over time, the difficulties in attacking communication targets meant the secondary part of this directive, and its stipulated city targets that included Hamburg and Bremen, assumed greater importance, taking centre stage in British bombing policy in February 1942.

Hamburg, viewed as containing large numbers of industrial workers as well as naval and railway targets, saw five attacks in the four weeks after 9 July. Operations on 16–17 and 25–26 July were smaller than planned, bad weather having prevented sending a larger force, whilst a daylight raid on 26 July was by two Fortresses from 2 Group. Peirse sent forces of 80 and 44 aircraft on 2–3 and 8–9 August respectively, the aiming points being railway stations and marshalling yards, around which lay plenty of workers' houses. Yet the age-old problem remained of locating these facilities. Such difficulties were, of course, widespread – something which the Butt Report had exposed – but Peirse maintained the effort against Hamburg with six attacks in September and October. Perhaps a marginally easier city to locate than many others, being along the Elbe, Ultra also revealed the pocket battleship *Admiral Scheer* was to arrive at the Blohm & Voss shipyard for 'certain work' on 28 September. Peirse's diary entry for the operation two nights later describes 'many bursts' being observed around 'the quay where the Adml Scheer was lying'.

Many airmen perceived operations to Hamburg had become tougher by this time. The 405 (RCAF) Squadron Wellington containing navigator and bomb aimer Sergeant J.A. Wymark was caught in the city's searchlights on 15–16 September. The Canadian pilot violently corkscrewed, causing Wymark, lying prone over the bomb sight, to be unable to move 'because the G-force against me meant you were stuck to the floor'. The night fighters seemed more lethal, too. New Zealander Sergeant J.A. Ward and crew were intercepted on their homeward journey. Exiting the burning Wellington, Canadian navigator Flight Sergeant L.E. Peterson later recalled:

About 15–20 miles out of Hamburg, a night fighter attacked … from port with cannon and [machine-gun fire]. Aircraft was immediately a mass of flames … and [I] opened the door for [the] front gunner, and he and I baled out by parachute. While I was coming down I saw the aircraft go down and hit the ground, in flames.

This operation damaged three U-boats at Blohm & Voss and sank a ship carrying iron ore from Scandinavia, whilst a 4,000lb bomb landed squarely on a testing shed at Howaldtswerke, causing the loss of 20 submarine engines. The city authorities revealed 76 deaths and damage to houses in the districts of Harvesterhuder and Uhlenhorst, around the northern end of Lake Alster, damage that carried sinister implications for the city's Jewish population.

On 20 October, the War Cabinet, at the Admiralty's request, told Bomber Command to revert to attacking Battle of the Atlantic targets. Bottomley instructed Peirse that although transportation and morale remained the primary targets, Hamburg, Kiel, Bremen and Wilhelmshaven were 'high-priority' targets in good weather because of their U-boat production. These naval targets, the C-in-C was told, were to be attacked using 'your present principle of following up a successful attack with subsequent concentrations as closely spaced as weather conditions permit'. Peirse bombed Hamburg on 26–27 October and five nights later, with the first effort causing damage to two floating docks and the destroyer and U-boat being fitted out in them. Pathfinder legend John Searby remembered the second attack vividly. Posted to 405 (RCAF) Squadron, he flew a 'second dicky' trip in the Wellington of New Zealander Sergeant E.J. Williams. With the weather deteriorating at the German coast, they descended to 4,000ft to ascertain their whereabouts – which allowed light flak guns to open up. 'The stuff whizzed past the Wellington … close and nasty, and one of which might have done for us all,' Searby recalled. The determined Williams merely continued, climbing to 10,000ft once his navigator had determined their location. In so doing, the Wellington went straight into a huge thundercloud, where lightning flashed continuously and the upcurrent 'tossed the Wellington around the sky in the most sick-making fashion'. After bombing the target, Williams evaded intense flak by climbing and standing the Wellington on its tail before pushing 'the stick … forward and [making] … a steep dive turning out toward the coast'. Holding the Wellington's nose down until the airframe began 'shaking violently', further aerial aerobics commenced to avoid the light flak guarding the Elbe estuary. 'Sorry about the rough stuff,' Williams sardonically stated upon clambering out from the landed Wellington. Searby was impressed by the New Zealander's determination to press on.

Losses on these two raids were 3.5 per cent and 3.2 per cent respectively (four aircraft each); a further attack by 103 aircraft on 9–10 November saw just one Wellington lost (0.9 per cent), the unlucky one being that of Pilot Officer H.V. Wilgar-Robinson from 9 Squadron. These were favourable loss rates, well below the 5 per cent benchmark for operations, but they were not the norm. Two nights previously had seen the heaviest casualty rates of all,

Air Chief-Marshal Sir Richard Peirse. Arguably the unlucky head of Bomber Command (from 5 October 1940–8 January 1942), around long enough to be blamed for the increasingly ineffective performances and sluggish expansion of the bomber force but possessing too short a tenure to benefit from the navigation aids soon appearing. 'When you attacked me yesterday evening for developing so small a force for night bombing', he wrote to Churchill on 27 April 1941, 'I admit you got me on the raw because not only am I very conscious of the smallness of my available resources, but also because I have in fact worked them as hard as their numbers and weather permit, until in fact each Group Commander has asked me to ease up'. (EN-Archive)

when a force attacking Berlin suffered 12.4 per cent casualties, 13 per cent were lost on the accompanying attack to Mannheim and small forces on roving operations to the Ruhr and minelaying near Oslo endured 21 per cent losses. Summoned to Chequers on 8 November for an explanation, it spelt the end of Peirse's leadership of Bomber Command; he left two months later. In the meantime, he was informed about the War Cabinet's decision regarding 'the necessity for conserving our resources in order to build a strong force to be available by the spring of next year'. What became known as the Conservation Order was applied over the following months, with limitations placed on Bomber Command's operations against Germany. Losses fell to 2.4 per cent and helped the Command's numerical recovery, although some of the sporadic attacks on Germany could still be expensive. On 30 November–1 December, Peirse sent 181 bombers to attack Hamburg, of which 13 aircraft (7.2 per cent) failed to return. Already a difficult year for Bomber Command, 1941 had ended badly, and a six-month bureaucratic battle for the bomber force's survival lay ahead, with its effectiveness questioned by most and its aircraft desired by many. The glimmers of hope – the Lancaster, Mosquito, Gee navigation device and Sir Arthur Harris – could not come soon enough.

The raids of 1942

Despite being in the doldrums during winter 1941–42, Bomber Command would not leave the city and people of Hamburg alone. Under Air Vice-Marshal J.E.A. Baldwin, the temporary C-in-C following Peirse's departure, a double attack was made on 14–15 and 15–16 January. The first attack started some fires, with one being particularly large in a dockside timber yard, whilst the second, co-ordinated with an attack on Emden, was hampered by cloud over the target. Taking shelter during the first attack, a Swedish seaman told British intelligence the occupants were 'more concerned' by 'whether "an aerial torpedo or mine" might fall than anything else', which confirmed the belief that the larger blast bomb, especially the 4,000lb 'cookie', proved a major strain on civilian nerves.

The area bombing of Germany's industrial cities was enshrined in the directive sent by Bottomley on 14 February, which Harris inherited following his arrival at HQ Bomber Command eight days later. This directive remained in force throughout 1942, only superseded by the Casablanca Directive on 4 February 1943. Targets in the Ruhr were listed as 'the most important', whose closer proximity to the UK allowed the use of Gee, but the directive listed diversions, 'the destruction of which is of immediate importance in the light of the current strategical situation'. This comprised building yards in Hamburg and Kiel, and reflected the wider concern over the U-boat menace at this time. In January 1942, some 250 U-boats operated, set to experience their second 'happy time' off America's East Coast and the Caribbean. On 3 April, Harris sent a paper titled 'Bomber Command's Contribution to the Anti-Submarine Campaign' to Churchill, arguing 'the best way' to attack them was at source, in other words the building yards in Germany. April 1942 saw four raids on Rostock, which contained the Neptunwerft building yards, two attacks on Hamburg and one raid on the Deutsche Werft shipyards in Kiel. Blending several elements, HQ Bomber Command's operation order to the Groups for attacking *Dace* stated the aim was 'to cause max. dam. to industrial centre [and] … to cause max. destruct. to a shipyard', although tellingly it also emphasized 'the primary target is aiming point in the centre of the old town'. Doing this, it was hoped, would catch everything within the given area that was considered worth bombing.

Thus, on 8–9 April, a maximum effort of 272 aircraft – including seven Lancasters – took off to bomb Hamburg. Encountering electrical storms and severe icing, there was 'no photographic evidence to suggest that this raid achieved any success', the final raid report noted, because 'none of the seven photographs taken are within 5 miles of the target and three of these have been plotted between 30 and 75 miles from it'. Nine nights later, a forecast predicting 'excellent weather' saw another maximum effort made. However, the continual problem of navigation was revealed by just two of the 22 night photographs showing the target – one aircraft getting to the Deutsche Werke shipyard and dropping its 4,000lb bomb that probably went into the Elbe – and another two were plotted within 5 miles of the target. From 178 aircraft despatched, 39 aborted, 32 bombed targets in German-occupied territory and 107 claimed an attack but quite where remained anyone's guess. The message was clear: the problems highlighted by the Butt Report very much remained, even against supposedly easier-to-find Hamburg. Much improvement would be needed – and made – to allow Bomber Command to inflict the devastation of Operation *Gomorrah* just 15 months later.

Bombs are hoisted into a Wellington on 15 January 1942 for that night's operation to Hamburg. (Getty Images)

The Hamburg operation on 3–4 May, occurring right before the 100th anniversary of the great fire of 1842, was by a small force of 81 bombers. Ultra decrypted a report by the Turkish Ambassador in Berlin which stated the northern districts were 'completely destroyed', with the population going into the streets in a mood of 'bewilderment and fear'. Some confirmation was provided by the *Hamburger Fremdenblatt*, which reported that 'almost without exception all bombs hit densely populated residential districts', and photographs on 7 May revealed damage in the city. It would be incorrect to say a great improvement in navigation had facilitated this outcome, however. Aircrews admitted to releasing their bombs on ETA or a timed run from the Elbe estuary, and on this occasion Bomber Command had simply been lucky in the bombs dropping in the right place.

Poor operational performance provided evidence for yet another investigation into Bomber Command's effectiveness. The Singleton Report's conclusions were not positive, ending with the gloomy prognosis: 'I do not think that great results can be hoped for within six months.' Summer 1942 therefore saw Harris' unwritten aim of achieving favourable headlines for the Command and accounts for the 1,000-bomber attacks on Cologne (the first choice being Hamburg before poor weather forced the switch) and Essen in late May and early June. Buoyed by the *Millennium* operations, he sent his views on future targeting strategy in a lengthy paper to Churchill, opening with the hardly subtle line of 'Victory, speedy and complete, awaits the side which first employs air power as it should be employed', which was against the enemy's population centres. On the campaign against the U-boat, Harris dismissed Coastal Command as doing 'nothing essential … [but] search[ing] for the needle in the haystack'. In contrast, if heavy bomber production was given the highest priority Harris promised Bomber Command would 'progressively' and 'utterly' destroy Bremen, Bremerhaven, Wilhelmshaven, Hamburg and Kiel, before going on to 'wreck' the Ruhr and Berlin.

These were bold claims, and it was immediately necessary for Harris to demonstrate that such objectives could be achieved. In July, considerable shipping, especially oil tankers, was observed in Hamburg, whilst the city's shipyards saw eight tank landing craft and 24 U-boats being fitted out. Several covered slips and two concrete submarine pens were noted as being nearly 'completely roofed', and construction of Hamburg's flak towers was continuing 'rapidly'. Expected to be soon operational for defending the very shipyards where 30 per cent of Germany's U-boats were produced, HQ Bomber Command believed Hamburg needed to be re-attacked. A force of 403 aircraft, which would have been larger had strong winds not cancelled the OTUs' (Operational Training Units') participation, set out on 26–27 July. Reflecting Bomber Command's evolving tactics, the aim was to saturate the city's air defences

Großadmiral Karl Dönitz, Hitler's successor and architect of U-Boat warfare in the Atlantic, and Albert Speer, Minister for Arms and War Production. When Dönitz replaced Raeder as head of the Germany Navy in early 1943, he secured Speer's assistance on naval production but, in doing so, allowed submarine design to follow the bureaucrats' wishes, particularly those of Otto Merker, for making the prefabricated U-Boats. Much time and resources were lost on producing a weapon that was ultimately a great failure. Throughout 1944, however, Dönitz held great hopes of restarting the campaign against Allied shipping with these new models of submarine and older ones fitted with the *Schnorkel* device. '[N]ew successes were within our grasp' Dönitz wrote in his memoirs, but it ultimately was not to be. (EN-Archive)

by compressing the attack into 45 minutes. With the entire bomber force organized in three sections, the first part, attacking from 0100hrs to 0120hrs, contained the best crews carrying the maximum amount of 4lb incendiaries; the second bombed from 0115hrs to 0135hrs and also carried large incendiary loads; and the third, attacking from 0130hrs to 0145hrs, carried the high explosives. On a clear night, 78 per cent of the force claimed to have attacked Hamburg – perceived by some aircrews as lit up like 'a second Cologne' – but later evidence proved otherwise. From 135 night photographs, just 70 were plotted within 5 miles of the city centre, a statistic that showed Bomber Command was hardly a remorseless machine of efficiency. Worse still was the loss rate of 7.2 per cent (29 aircraft). Heavy concentrations of searchlights operating with flak batteries shot down 12 bombers and damaged another 45 aircraft. The 408 (RCAF) Squadron Hampden of Pilot Officer David Williams had finished its bomb run at 8,000ft when heavy flak shells burst underneath the port wing, blowing the aircraft onto its back, and only desperate action to restart the engines allowed the aircraft to right itself. Night fighters made 55 interceptions, with 20 developing into combats, culminating in eight bombers shot down, one being the 106 Squadron Lancaster of Squadron Leader F.H. Robertson which fell victim to Leutnant Lothar Linke (II–NJG-1). Pilot Officer P.N. Rayne's Hampden (420 Squadron) was attacked by a night fighter near Tönning, along the German coast, which set it ablaze. Ordering the crew to jump, Rayne's account reveals how desperate his own escape was:

[T]he next thing I realised was that [the] a–c was diving to the ground and that there were flames all round me which burnt my protected face. I tried to release my harness but could not find the pin nor see anything … . After several unsuccessful attempts I suddenly found myself loose; I stood up & was sucked out of the diving a–c.

The repeat attack resulted in just a handful of fires in Hamburg, the meagre outcome of an operation that had descended into a shambles. Bad weather had cancelled aircraft from 1, 4 and 5 Groups and training units of 92 and 93 Groups, but 165 aircraft from 3 Group and 91 OTU still took off. Encountering thunderstorms, many aborted, and in the end just 70 hopelessly scattered aircraft carried on to Germany, where air defences picked off 11.3 per cent of the force. Things were especially deadly over Hamburg. Covered to 14,000ft by 10–10ths cloud, above which lay the hazards of icing and bright moonlight that assisted prowling night fighters, many bombers descended to clearer conditions to see the city; in so doing, their aircraft became silhouetted against the light grey cloud above them and lower-flying night fighters shot down nine bombers. Becoming known as 'Baldwin's Folly' because the former temporary C-in-C had pressed on at 3 Group's expense, which he now led, 75 (NZ) Squadron had a dreadful night, losing six Wellingtons. Sergeant C. Croall's aircraft suffered flak damage over Hamburg that weakened its structure and, with no warning, the tail fell off, killing the rear gunner, the remaining part of the aircraft just being able to ditch off the German coast. Squadron Leader Richard Kearns recalled that 'there was almost a riot' on the squadron afterwards: 'You felt as though you had been let down very badly by the powers-that-be.' Kearns himself had a very hectic operation, only escaping Hamburg's searchlights by flying down to treetop level, going 'under three sets of power lines' and letting the gunners blaze away at flak and searchlight installations. The other unit that really suffered was 3 Group's training formation, 1651 HCU (Heavy Conversion Unit), which lost four Stirlings containing experienced instructors and novice crews.

Vickers Wellington, a regular participant in Bomber Command's operations against Hamburg from June 1940 to July 1943. Pictured are Mk.Is from 9 Squadron early in the war (Getty Images)

Overall, this pointed to a trend of increasing operational losses. Night fighters increasingly operated in pairs, one to distract the air gunners whilst the other sneaked up from the rear quarter to deliver the usually fatal attack. Vast amounts of manpower and material had poured into the Kammhuber Line, allowing its expansion and deepening, whilst major targets had increasingly strong air defences. Together, these were delivering results: in late August, Harris lost 31 aircraft (10.1 per cent) against Kassel, and 11 per cent went missing on the dual attack on Nuremburg and Saarbrücken the following night. Portal told Churchill that with the Germans 'evidently concentrating their defences round their major towns … causing us increasing losses of night bombers', Harris wanted to attack smaller towns 'to achieve some dispersal of the [air] defences'. The bombing offensive against Germany hardly looked in great shape in autumn 1942. On 3 September, when Harris told Churchill that 'bombing … can be decisive' if Bomber Command could 'raze substantially to the ground 30–40 of the principal German cities', the prime minister was understandably not convinced.

During the rest of 1942, Hamburg received four attacks of varying size. Three Mosquitoes were simply designed to harass the city and its people on 18 September; the following day, another six Mosquitoes set out to bomb Berlin, but two dropped bombs on Hamburg instead. On 13–14 October, the target was Kiel, but many attacked Hamburg either in error or as an alternative target. By early November, intelligence revealed Dönitz's U-boat fleet was expanding, with 205 in operation and 130 in production, and under Churchill the Anti-U-Boat Committee was formed to organize the British response. Although committed to bombing Italy at this time, Harris, eager to retain the prime minister's confidence, despatched 213 aircraft against Hamburg on 9–10 November, notwithstanding three weather conferences being held. One at 1620hrs saw the weather over Hamburg described as 'doubtful', with 5–10–10ths cloud and ground haze; the last, indicating continual poor weather, came whilst the bombers were taking off. Perhaps frustrated at the long period of inactivity over Germany, Harris did not recall the aircraft. He took a gamble – and promptly lost. Thick layers of cloud, with heavy icing, were experienced. Identification and marking of the aiming point – this being the Pathfinders'

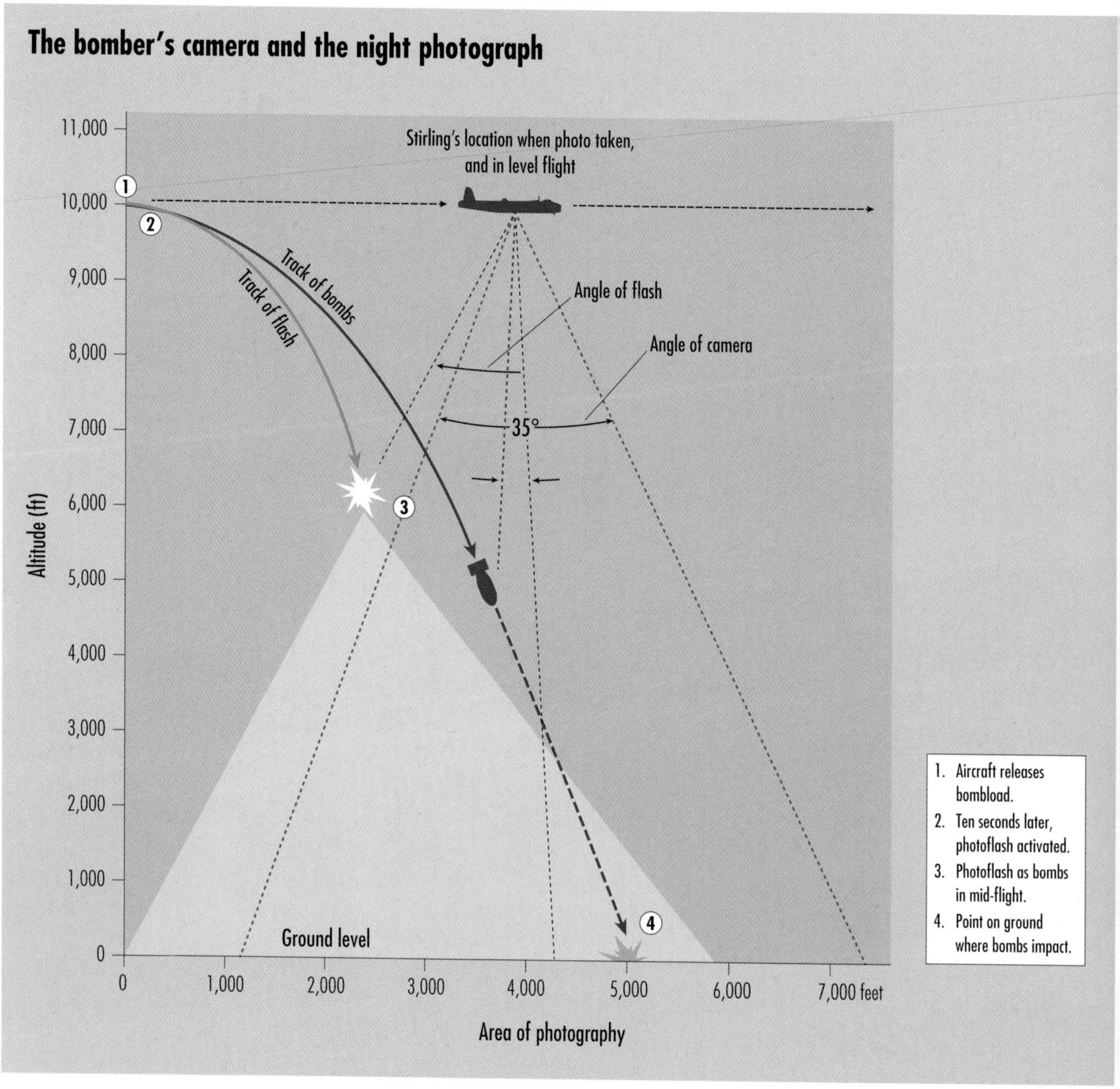
The bomber's camera and the night photograph
Stirling's location when photo taken, and in level flight
11,000
10,000
9,000
8,000
7,000
6,000
5,000
4,000
3,000
2,000
1,000
0
Altitude (ft)
Track of bombs
Track of flash
Angle of flash
Angle of camera
35°
Ground level
0
1,000
2,000
3,000
4,000
5,000
6,000
7,000 feet
Area of photography
1. Aircraft releases bombload.
2. Ten seconds later, photoflash activated.
3. Photoflash as bombs in mid-flight.
4. Point on ground where bombs impact.

ABOVE THE BOMBER'S CAMERA AND THE NIGHT PHOTOGRAPH

This diagram shows how the ideal night photograph was taken by a bomber, in which the pilot had to maintain a straight and level course. Yet the hot nature of Bomber Command's targets, with flak, searchlights and night fighters in abundance, meant great nerve was required to do this. Should the pilot be compelled to bank or dive to dodge the defences, or indeed be over eager to get away from the target area, then the photograph would be taken whilst the bomber was manoeuvring. This would be inaccurate as the photography would not show the situation vertically below the bomber, but off to the left or right, whilst if diving, the photograph would be of the situation behind the aircraft, not directly below. The process for taking accurate night photographs comprised:

0: Flying straight and level, the bomb aimer presses the button to release the bomb load; simultaneously the camera's flash is also released.

0–24secs: Two frames are loaded into the camera with an additional one in place for the exposure. In the cockpit a red light glows for two seconds informing the pilot to hold the aircraft level.

25–31secs: Flash explodes and two night photographs are taken.

32–36secs: The pilot's red light glows once again meaning the process has been completed; he can now bank the aircraft away from the target area.

first operation to Hamburg – was unsuccessful. The Main Force instead released its bombs based on ETA from route markers dropped by the PFF at the southern end of Lake Ratzeburger, some 32 miles east-by-north-east of Hamburg. With Gee largely unavailable because of German jamming, navigators resorted to astro fixes, but changes in wind direction hampered everything. Not surprisingly, German records noted just a handful of houses were hit and a few industrial buildings 'slightly affected'. Despite promises of shattering U-boat production centres, this was hardly looking believable. Harris was confronted by another attack on Hamburg going wrong. It was proving a frustrating target, and an expensive one too. Fifteen aircraft (7.1 per cent) failed to return; ten lost to 'causes unknown' (probably icing), four to flak and one to night fighters.

Inside the U-Boat pens at Finkenwärder following an attack by the 'special' bombs of Bomber Command. The light shining in from the roof, and the bent steel rods, indicate this part of the roof took a direct hit. (Getty Images)

Attacked eight times during 1942, the results on Hamburg, Harris described to Lovett, 'are satisfactory as far as they go', but 'if the attack is maintained and intensified they may be catastrophic in 1943'. Nonetheless, in such a short space of time, a lot needed to be done before attacks on Hamburg could be accurately described as catastrophic. In the meantime, the bombing commitment against the U-boat went in the opposite direction towards their bases at Brest, Lorient, St Nazaire and La Pallice, which was only terminated in April 1943.

The battle of the German ports, January–April 1943

By January 1943, the U-Boat arm, as Allied intelligence well knew, had expanded considerably. Twelve months before, the Kriegsmarine had 91 operational U-boats, 158 undergoing training and another 96 being built. Now, the number available for war operations had increased by 133 per cent to 212, whilst another 181 were undergoing sea trials and 69 were being constructed. Moreover, 30 January 1943 saw a man utterly dedicated to prosecuting submarine warfare in the Atlantic appointed as C-in-C of the German Navy, namely Großadmiral Karl Dönitz. He soon agreed to place U-boat construction under Speer's ministry in return for the monthly production being increased from 20 to 40 submarines.

Battle of the North German Ports, 30–31 January–20–21 April 1943				
Target	Date	Bomb loads	Aircraft despatched	Aircraft lost
Hamburg	30–31 January	339	148	5
	3–4 February	394	263	16
	3–4 March	922	417	10
TOTAL:		1,655	828	31 (3.7 per cent)
Wilhelmshaven	11–12 February	432	177	3
	18–19 February	596	195	4
	19–20 February	782	338	11
	24–25 February	192	115	0
TOTAL:		2,002	825	18 (2.1 per cent)
Kiel	4–5 April	1,381	577	13 (2.2 per cent)
Stettin	20–21 April	848	339	22 (6.5 per cent)
Bremen	21–22 February	424	143	0
TOTAL:		6,310	2,712	84 (3.1 per cent)

The burning buildings during Hamburg's Firestorm of 27–28 July 1943. Senior SS and police leader, Georg Henning Graf von Bassewitz-Behr, likened the effect to Mt Vesuvius' destruction of Pompeii. (EN-Archive)

Hamburg was attacked by Bomber Command three times in early 1943. The first occasion was on 30–31 January, marking the beginning of an air campaign against Germany's major ports lasting some 11 weeks. It represented a particular landmark in the operational history of Bomber Command, for H2S was used for identifying and marking the aiming point for the first time. Choosing Hamburg to debut this device was no coincidence; it was relatively easy to find and had geographical features H2S was expected to outline, namely its large river and distinctive tributaries, around which was the equally distinctive harbour area. In practice, H2S as a device for blind bombing made an indifferent start. Installed in just 13 Pathfinder Stirlings and Halifaxes, bad weather saw four PFF aircraft turn back, while another three had trouble with their devices. Although the aiming point at the southern end of the Binnenalster lake was marked accurately, the lack of H2S-equipped PFF aircraft meant the marking was not consistently maintained, and thus the Main Force's bombing became scattered, especially when increasing cloud forced a switch to H2S-led sky marking. Some damage was inflicted to the Blohm & Voss and Deutsche Werft shipyards, several oil tanks, some merchant ships docked along the Petersen Kai and a railway bridge across the Elbe. The night fighters also had an indifferent night, in which 71 GCI sorties yielded just two interceptions, resulting in one bomber being shot down. Three others succumbed to flak, including one that blew up in mid-air over Bremen, and another to causes unknown.

An attack on Hamburg (or alternatively Essen) was set for 1–2 February, but both raids were cancelled due to poor weather. Two nights later, the forecast seemed little better as heavy cloud gathered over the North Sea and Hamburg, but the operation went ahead. Electrical storms and icing were encountered at 22,000ft, and from a force of 263 bombers, just 126 aircraft attacked the target. The dense cloud over the target saw sky marking used, but this method hardly worked properly when just five from 11 PFF aircraft reached the target, with the remainder succumbing to various technical defects caused by the extreme cold – engines, a rear turret and – most significantly – inoperable H2S sets. Many Main Force crews saw little and dropped their bombs on the glows of fires lurking beneath the thick clouds. Some hits, more from luck than anything else, were inflicted on three building slips at Blohm & Voss and the U-boats being constructed on them. Some optimism came from H2S operators reporting Hamburg's response as clear, with the Elbe and dock area being recognizable. Sixteen aircraft (6.1 per cent) were missing, however. Eight were victim to the terrible conditions, with a number probably spinning out of control due to icing, and four were shot down by the Bf.110s from NJG-1. That unit lost experienced ace Hauptmann Reinhold Knacke when the Halifax he shot down also downed his night fighter, and both machines crashed near to each other in Holland. Although thick cloud hampered the searchlights, considerable amounts of flak were fired into the sky, especially where the Pathfinders dropped route markers, namely the turning points at Hoya and Wenzendorf, the latter representing the start of the final run into Hamburg. Flak gunners shot down four bombers – one being the 408 (RCAF) Squadron Halifax II of Flight Lieutenant W.A. Black which was hit in the fuel tanks, causing multiple engine failures and fire to break out – and damaging 18 others.

On 11 February, in a speech to the House of Commons on the war situation, Churchill stated that 'the defeat of the U-boat' was 'the prelude to all effective aggressive operations'. Harris continued attacking building yards throughout the month, bombing Wilhelmshaven four times and Bremen once. Post-raid photography of Cologne, taken after the 26–27

February raid, showed the Humboldt-Deutz plant, which made diesel engines for U-boats, had been set on fire. Bomber Command launched a large attack against Hamburg on 3–4 March, with 417 aircraft detailed for the raid. However, the final attack on Hamburg before *Gomorrah* resulted in a desperately poor outcome, notwithstanding good weather. Although 344 reported attacking the target, few bomb loads landed in the right place. Looking at evidence from the night photographs, just seven were plotted within 3 miles of the aiming point (the Altona railway station), another five between 3 and 5 miles away, 105 somewhere beyond this and an eye-watering 172 over an unknown location (see pages 64–65 to reveal what exactly went wrong). What was clear, however, was that stronger opposition was encountered on this night. A Polish crew in a Wellington fought off two Ju.88s and downed one, a Halifax rear gunner shot down an Me.110 and another Halifax outmanoeuvred the successive attacks of a Ju.88 and two Me.110s. At 103 Squadron, having just returned from leave, Flight Sergeant Don Charlwood of the Royal Australian Air Force (RAAF) recalled meeting his returned colleagues, with one reporting: 'Chopberg seems to get progressively hotter; bags of flak and plenty of fighters.' Others thought the heavy flak was less intense, but this was symptomatic of aircraft not being over Hamburg but much further to the west.

Two nights later, Harris opened the Battle of the Ruhr. Nevertheless, destroying Hamburg remained in Portal's mind. When Harris submitted a letter of protest on 6 March about the number and 'inconsistency' of the directives he had been receiving since November 1942, the CAS told Bottomley:

I don't understand what the C in C has to complain about. He is given tremendous latitude for 9–10ths of his bombing and it is up to him to concentrate his effort as much as weather allows. What his directive really means is that he should obliterate Hamburg, Bremen and Kiel as quickly as possible & that when weather does not allow attacks on these cities he should go for others of the highest industrial value with a preference for those which are important in the U–Boat & Aircraft Industries.

Indeed, Portal wrote to Harris the following day requesting 'an explanation of the reason why we are not at present time doing half the number of raids with double the strength in each'. Nonetheless, to stem any criticism, the CAS stated that 'if you can pull off an 800 raid on a place such as Hamburg, I shall be delighted', a size of force nearly equivalent to the number despatched on four occasions during Operation *Gomorrah* four months later. Harris selected Hamburg (with Cologne as an alternative) for attack on 25–26 March, but a poor forecast saw its cancellation at 1330hrs.

Meanwhile, at a meeting of the Air Ministry's Targets Committee on 9 April, the Coastal Command representative wished 'to draw attention to the good effects that a night blitz on Hamburg, combined with a daylight attack on the submarine yards, should have on the Battle of the Atlantic'. Bufton, the committee's chairman, agreed, stating that 'Hamburg was No.1 priority and that the Americans and Bomber Command intended to attack this target as, and when, tactical and other considerations allowed'. Such views hastened HQ Bomber Command's planning over forthcoming weeks for Hamburg's destruction, guided by 'NAVTAR' (Naval Targets), issued every two weeks by Bufton's committee. Sent on a 'purely informative' basis, probably because the Air Staff were keen to avoid further disagreements erupting between Harris and the Navy, NAVTARs stated 'the current order of priority of specific targets within the general class[es] of naval targets' as recommended by the Admiralty. In first place came U-boat building yards, and within this category, the NAVTARs issued throughout May placed Hamburg as the priority target.

Operationally, April witnessed continued attacks on the Ruhr, alongside Frankfurt, Stuttgart, Pilsen, Mannheim and the ports of Kiel, Rostock and Stettin. The latter, raided by 339

Missing the target: the Hamburg Operation, 3–4 March 1943

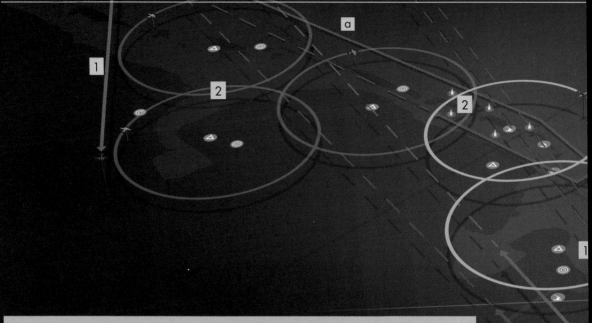

EVENTS

1. 19.00 to 20.30hrs: British bomber formation (417 aircraft) approaches the north-west coast of Germany. 14 heavy bombers from 3 and 4 Groups drop 30 mines around the Frisian Islands and five Mosquitoes test Oboe in the Ruhr.

2. 20.15hrs: German radars detect incoming British formations; GCI night fighters take off to patrol the Kammhuber Line. British forces deploy Tinsel which hampers ground-controlled night fighters.

3. 20.30hrs: a Pathfinder drops a white route-marker near Husum; aircraft from 7 and 35 Squadrons drop a marker when passing. At the target, seven mark the aiming-point with a red T.I. 19 'back-up' aircraft from 8 Group, drop green T.I.s at the centre of the red T.I.s. Only eight reach the target with the Y-apparatus serviceable.

4. 20.30 to 21.00hrs: the British formation encounters lively flak and searchlight defences at Husum. One British aircraft is shot down.

5. 21.00 to 21.15hrs: weak Gee signals cause a Pathfinder to follow the Elbe to the assumed target; 'where river narrows' and drops its red T.I.s at Wedel. One aircraft marks the aiming-point correctly, whilst the next drops markers between the two areas of red T.I.s.

6. 21.00 to 21.15hrs: the aircraft following the Elbe drops a yellow route-marker 15 miles from the target taking the Main Force away from Altona; red markers there are believed to be a German diversion. The Germans activate their decoy site near Wedel; a stream damned to produce a lake similar to the Aussenalster; many aircrew are deceived.

7. 21.15hrs: three distinct areas of red ground-markers established; one at the correct aiming-point (the Altona railway station), one at Wedel, and another somewhere in between. Owing to the misplacing of the yellow route-marker, the Wedel concentration is seen first by most Main Force crews.

8. 21.15 to 21.50hrs: many bombs fall onto the villages of Wedel, Schulau and Risse. Very little damage in Hamburg, only 17 aircraft have dropped their bombs within three miles of the 'real' aiming-point in Altona.

9. 21.10 to 22.00hrs: intense activity by 200 searchlights in the Hamburg area. Flak is fired but only mild anti-aircraft fire is encountered. Flak shoots down three bombers over north-west Hamburg.

10. 2100 to 2240hrs: night fighters are operating, but British jamming hinders the German effort. Only nine attacks are reported. Just ten aircraft are lost, due to the bomber-stream being concentrated. Three German night fighters are shot down.

11. 21.50 to 22.25hrs: the bomber-stream, by now scattered, crosses the heavily defended coastal areas and flak brings down one. AA and searchlight defences on the eastern Frisian Islands, and Heligoland are assisted by several flak-ships and damage another seven aircraft.

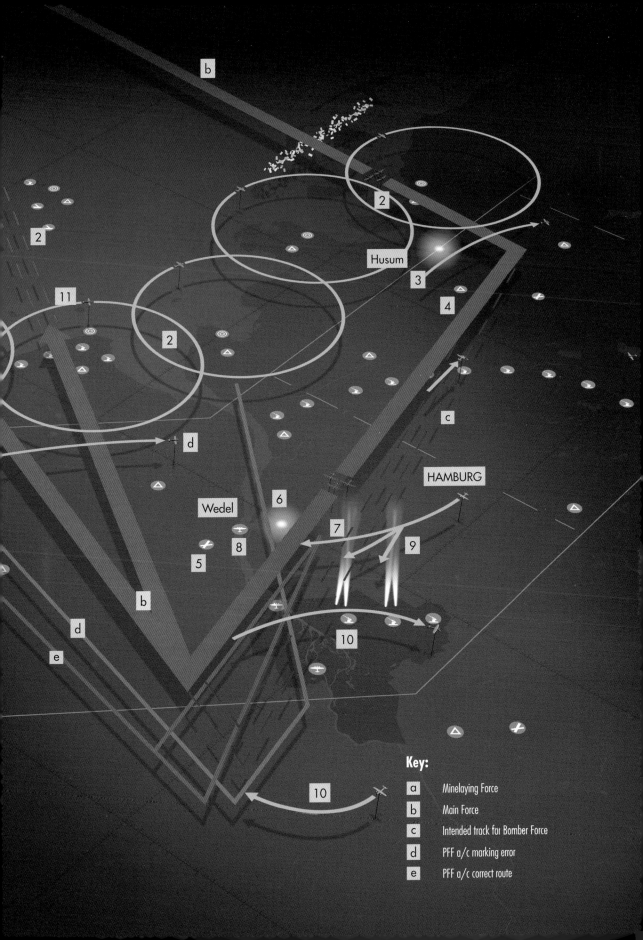

b

2

11

2

2

Husum

3

4

c

d

HAMBURG

Wedel

6

7

9

5

8

10

b

d

e

10

Key:

a	Minelaying Force
b	Main Force
c	Intended track for Bomber Force
d	PFF a/c marking error
e	PFF a/c correct route

The morning after Hamburg's Firestorm of 27–28 July 1943: rubble-strewn streets, burning buildings but people still going about their business. (Getty Images)

aircraft on 20–21 April, was particularly successful, with some 100 acres of Stettin being destroyed. HQ Bomber Command was particularly pleased because it showed H2S could deliver accurate marking and a destructive attack. They also observed how the level of damage stemmed from an overstretched fire service becoming overwhelmed early in the attack – a development vitally important for what transpired at Hamburg some 12 weeks later. Meanwhile, an attack on Hamburg on 13–14 April, although very small in nature, was a landmark raid because non-Oboe Mosquitoes from 2 Group made their first nuisance raid. Such attacks would become a perpetual irritation to the Germans for the rest of the war.

On 27 May, HQ Bomber Command sent the groups the order for Operation *Gomorrah*, which clearly stated the aim was to destroy the city of Hamburg in a series of attacks. On 16 June, Harris told Portal that, following the completion of the Battle of the Ruhr, the intention was to take apart industrial Germany. He wrote:

> As the nights lengthen out we will then go progressively further into Germany in I hope sufficient strength to be able to leave behind us, as we progress, a state of devastation similar to that now obtaining in the Ruhr; if the Boche waits for it. We shall then have available to us more plums in the way of objectives such as the complete destruction of Hamburg.

The countdown to 'the complete destruction of Hamburg' soon began. Harassing raids, comprising four Mosquitoes on each occasion, were made on 26–27 and 28–29 June and 3–4 and 5–6 July. These occurred simultaneously with the destruction caused to another German city in a concentrated series of raids, namely Cologne. Enduring three major attacks in nine nights by forces of 608, 653 and 282 aircraft, the city suffered particularly acutely from the second raid on 3–4 July, which left fires burning furiously the following day. Harris shifted the aiming point from its western side across the Rhine to Cologne's eastern districts – where the Gottfried-Hagen and Humboldt-Deutz factories making U-boat batteries and diesel engines respectively were situated – to ensure devastation throughout. The Air Ministry's final assessment emphasized that 'the completeness of the catastrophe' in Cologne was precisely down to repeat attacks having been made in quick succession. Industrial damage was 'immense', and 350,000 people, one-third of Cologne's population, had been de-housed. On 10 July, no doubt with Cologne's destruction in mind, Harris told Trenchard: 'I really feel that lately we have been getting somewhere.' It was an ominous precursor to Hamburg's impending fate, executed in a similar manner.

Operation *Gomorrah*, 24–25 July to 2–3 August 1943

According to Speer, sometime in 1940, Hitler rhetorically asked him:

> Have you ever looked at a map of London? It is so closely built up that one source of fire alone would suffice to destroy the whole city, as happened once before, two hundred years ago. Göring wants to use innumerable incendiary bombs of an altogether new type to create

sources of fire in all parts of London... Then they'll unite in one gigantic area conflagration [bringing the] ... total destruction of London. What use will their fire department be once that really starts!

In many ways this represented an accurate prediction of what befell Hamburg in summer 1943, when raging infernos burnt down some 70 per cent of the city. These were the attacks of Operation *Gomorrah*, a relatively short lived but extremely violent attack. In his diary, one airman wrote:

It is impressed on us [at briefing] that this is the big one... Crews are told that they must put Hamburg out of action and we will keep going night after night until we do... Next day we are on Ops. We are briefed for Hamburg... True to their word we are going back until we eliminate it.

Comprising four major attacks made between 24–25 July and 2–3 August, in total some 8,200 tons of bombs were dropped. HQ Bomber Command had calculated 10,000 tons were needed to destroy Hamburg; Harris had probably intended to make a fifth attack.

The first raid saw 791 bombers despatched, with 728 delivering an attack that opened at 0057hrs and lasted 53 minutes. Eleven Mosquitoes undertook harassing raids on Kiel, Duisburg, Bremen and Lübeck, and six Wellingtons sowed mines in the Elbe, no easy task given these required releasing at a low height within an area bristling with light flak AA guns. Called 'gardening' or 'vegetable planting', with the Elbe estuary codenamed *Eglantines*, minelaying here aimed to stop shipping and newly completed U-boats from leaving Hamburg's port. In good visibility, the Pathfinders opened the attack on Hamburg using H2S for undertaking Newhaven ground marking. The first two 'blind illuminators' dropped their markers short of the target, one being plotted 5½ miles away, although the remaining nine dropped them accurately, with one set being particularly close to the aiming point. The first visual marker dropped its red markers into the water of the dock, some 2 miles south-east of the aiming point over Altona, and simultaneously a second aircraft released its red markers about 1½ miles to the north-west. Others fell 3¼ miles east-by-north-east and 2½ miles west from where they should have been. Red target indicators were thus in four locations, around which some of the Main Force's first wave dropped their bombs. Eight minutes past the 01.00hrs zero-hour, the final red TI burnt out and responsibility for the attack now fell on the 'backers-up', who released green-coloured markers. Achieved successfully for seven minutes, undershooting by subsequent PFF aircraft saw considerable creep-back emerge, which 30 minutes into the attack meant 'a long carpet' of incendiaries now 'extended back along the line of approach for 7 miles in[4]. The marking performance on this attack was far from stellar, yet the sheer number of aircraft involved, coupled with the city's size, meant the record bomb tonnage – some 2,300 tons, beating the previous record of 2,000 tons released on Düsseldorf on 11–12 June – still fell on Hamburg, causing considerable damage. Luftwaffe day fighter pilot Oberfeldwebel Heinz Knoke, flying over the city on 25 July, observed 'great fires that are still raging everywhere in what has become a vast area of rubble', with the smoke plume standing out clearly against the blue summer sky, drifting eastward to the Baltic. '[T]he scene makes a deep impression on me', Knoke wrote, with the war now 'assuming some hideous aspects'.

The really 'hideous aspects' of area bombing came three nights later, however, when 787 bombers took off and inflicted the infamous 'firestorm' on the city. Confronted

4 From Bomber Command Report on Night Operations, 24/25th July 1943, 6/10/43. These were the official reports on each night operation produced by the Operational Research Section at HQ Bomber Command.

The 61 Squadron Lancaster of Pilot Officer W.H. Eager, RCAF, commences take-off on 29 July 1943, to participate in the third attack of Operation *Gomorrah*. The later USSBS found German documents saying this attack seemed 'the heaviest raid insofar as numbers of planes and bombs dropped are concerned'. (IWM CH 10675)

by some fires still burning from the opening attack, and smoke from two American raids, the Pathfinders' marking nonetheless was especially concentrated. Raging fires quickly engulfed the St Georg, Billwerder-Ausschlag, Barmbeck and Grasbrook districts, the city's water mains having been badly damaged in the first attack, and these numerous fires formed one huge conflagration. The hotter air above sucked in cooler air from below, assisted by draughts howling through already windowless and roofless buildings. Updraughts spread burning embers, creating further fires, and aircrews in the later waves felt the heat coming from 'a sea of flame', from which formed a gigantic smoke column rising to 22,000ft. Hamburg's inferno was observed for 200 miles on the return journey. These were 'cyclone-like firestorms', Speer wrote, and 'the asphalt of the streets began to blaze [and melt]' and people either 'burned to death in the streets' or were flung by violent winds into flaming buildings. Asphyxiation through lack of oxygen or carbon monoxide killed thousands in deathtrap cellars. The marking and timing followed that of the first raid (see pages 70-71), but greater concentration of the bomber stream allowed the raid to finish five minutes later. '[E]very such cut in the bombing period', 460 (RAAF) Squadron's ORB (Operations Record Book) noted, 'means greater destruction', and certainly pivotal to the devastating outcome was the sheer number of bombers that kept dropping their incendiaries on the well-concentrated target markers in the Billwerder district. Just 12 minutes into the raid, large fires blazed away in this area, serving to draw the following aircraft to this location. In total, the bombing pattern moved just 3½ miles east of the aiming point, a small distance when compared to Bomber Command's usual standard. Witnessing first hand Bomber Command's work was the commander of the US VIII Bomber Command, Brigadier-General Fred Anderson, who flew over Hamburg in the 83 Squadron Lancaster of Canadian Flight Lieutenant F.J. Garvey.

Anderson's bombers, reflecting long-standing American bombing doctrine (enshrined in the air plans AWPD-1 and AWPD-42), had attacked precision targets in the city – the shipyards of Blohm & Voss and Howaldtswerke and the Klöckner aero engine factory – on 25 and 26 July. For a fleeting moment, the CBO truly was a combined bombing offensive, with both strategic air forces attacking the same target. Yet practical difficulties had been revealed. Bomber Command's attack on 24–25 July, some 12 hours before the initial American raid, had left so much smoke the US aircrews could not see their targets, and their effort was spoilt. There would be no reruns in 1943 of the Anglo-American co-operation demonstrated over Hamburg, and indeed for the rest of the war such combined attacks remained the exception, not the norm.

Owing to a late take-off, this illustration depicts the aircraft of Sgt R.L. Henry, which was the 731st and last aircraft, bombing the suffering city on that night at 01.47a.m., several minutes after the attack had officially finished. The 427 Squadron ORB records Henry's aircraft dropping its bomb load in the Hammerbrook area of the city, at the 'centre of conflagration as no T.I. markers visible due to smoke and haze'. It also notes the crew saw an 'enormous column of smoke and large concentration of fires all around target', indicative of the firestorm growing in its maximum intensity. A huge smoke column had risen up to 22,000ft by the time Henry's crew attacked the target, which was 2,000ft higher than the altitude of Henry's aircraft. By this time, the city's air defences – as concentrated area bombing fully intended – had collapsed. 'Defences fell away almost to nothing towards the end of the attack', the official report noted, which were also badly affected by Bomber

Command's use of the Window countermeasure. Observing smoke some 45 miles away from Hamburg's still-burning fires, 8 Group led six waves of 777 bombers on the third attack on 29–30 July. In just 45 minutes, the vast bomb loads caused extensive devastation to Hamburg's north-eastern districts and port area. The post-raid report described the blind markers' yellow TIs as scattered some 2–3 miles east of the aiming point, and the backers'-ups green-TIs even worse at 3½ miles east-by-south-east of it. Again, the marking performance was far from good, yet concentrated bombing did materialize on undamaged areas, perhaps through luck as much as anything else. Later in the attack, 'an area of 24 square miles was covered with incendiaries'[5], accompanied by some massive explosions, including one at 0057hrs that was seen by aircrews 80 miles away. Those in the sixth wave reported this 'appeared to be the most successful of the three attacks'. The city authorities certainly believed so, labelling the destruction as 'gigantic', with the port heavily damaged and fires burning down the remaining parts of Barmbek.

In addition, three small-scale Mosquito harassing attacks were made, designed to both strain civilian nerves and assist the heavy attacks on Essen and Remscheid. As intended, the Luftwaffe remained focused on defending Hamburg and was fooled by the Mosquito 'spoof raid'; the main attack on Essen, in the past a very costly target, saw significantly lower casualties at 3.7 per cent. Another six Mosquitoes went to Hamburg on 26–27 July to maintain the pressure on the city, with four bombing the city centre and the remaining two releasing their bombs on Harburg. Four aircraft from 139 Squadron went two nights later, reporting the still-blazing fires 'made the target easily recognizable'.

Harris intended to make the fourth heavy attack on 30 July–1 August. Number 83 Squadron's ORB described how 'everything looked rosy' until 'a sudden thunderstorm broke, crews were in their aircraft waiting for permission to take off when the scrubb [*sic*] came through and there was a mad rush for the bar, to drown those blues'. The weather on 1 August was sufficiently clear, however, for photographic reconnaissance over Hamburg. HQ Bomber Command concluded that Wandsbek, Hammerbrock, Hamm, Horn and Bergfeld were practically eliminated, with Barmbek, Steilshoop, Uhlenforst and Winterhude very badly damaged. In total, 7 square miles of destruction was apparent throughout central and eastern Hamburg. Less-damaged areas were identified, however, particularly south of the Elbe. Consequently, 740 aircraft were sent to administer the *coup de grâce* on Hamburg on 2–3 August around two aiming points, one being in an undamaged part of the city centre and the other in the satellite town of Harburg.

What transpired was a farce not quite as bad as the Nuremburg disaster in March 1944, but somewhere near. Deciding to complete Hamburg's destruction before diversions took his bombers on to northern Italy and the V-2 facility at Peenemünde, on this occasion Harris pushed his crews over that fine margin between controlled risk and shambolic failure. The forecast predicted thunderstorms over north-west Germany and 'very doubtful' conditions at Hamburg; HQ Bomber Command's meteorological experts even recommended Kiel as 'slightly more favourable'. Air Vice-Marshal G.E. Brookes', AOC-in-C 6 Group, diary entry described 'much muttering re. weather', but the aircraft still took off, although 40 per cent of 6 Group's effort aborted due to icing. Many aircrews from other groups soon experienced solid 10–10ths anvil-shaped clouds up to 30,000ft, violent thunderstorms and severe lightning, heavy icing and intense static. '[B]lue electric flames' formed on the gun barrels, propellers and wing tips, reported one pilot from 460 Squadron, punctuated by 'the blinding flashes of lightning, very near to the aircraft'. Major J.K. Christie from 35 Squadron wrote of flying blindly into clouds 'shaken every ten seconds by terrific flashes which totally blinded me for many seconds afterwards'. Flying Officer Walter Thompson of

5   From Bomber Command Report on Night Operations, 29–30th July 1943, 11/10/43.

EVENTS

1. 21.15hrs to 22.30hrs: 787 aircraft take off to bomb Hamburg, land on the Schleswig coast and are attacked by German night fighters. The Lancaster of F/P L.R. Crampton (156 Squadron) crashes off Vollerwiek, also two RCAF Halifaxes near Neumünster, and the 102 Squadron Halifax of Sgt G.H. Brown near Rendsburg.

2. 23.25hrs to 00.05hrs: yellow route-markers are dropped in two locations across north-west Germany; the last one after Lübeck, the turning-point for the final approach to Hamburg from the E.N.E. Window is also released. The bomber-stream is divided into six waves, flying between 10,000 and 22,000ft.

3. 00.55hrs: 8 Group's aircraft begins the attack. The Pathfinders have 70 aircraft equipped with H2S.

4. 00.57hrs to 01.02hrs: 87 Main Force aircraft drop their bombs around the yellow target-markers in the Billwärder district, 1½ miles E.S.E. of Altstadt.

5. A force of six Wellingtons from 6 Group begins laying mines in the Elbe estuary.

6. 01.12hrs to 01.20hrs: large fires engulf the Billwärder-Ausschlag district, moving westwards into the central city area, then northwards.

7. Hamburg's air-defences, fighting blind because of Window, do their best. 17 (2.2%) of the bomber force are lost.

Flying a single-engine Bf.109 from *Wilde Sau* unit, I/JG-300, Major Hajo Herrmann shoots down the 101 Squadron Lancaster of F/Sgt D.P.P. Hurst, which crashes into the eastern suburbs. Ofw Wilhelm Kurreck downs the 102 Squadron Halifax of F/O G. McFarlane-Clarke, which crashes into the northern district of Sasel. Uffz Adolf Löschner fires on the 15 Squadron Stirling of F/L J.R. Childs. Hit by flak, the wounded bomber is then shot down and hits the ground at Ochsenwerder, near Harburg. Maj. Walter Ehle, having taken-off from St Trond in Belgium, attacks the 207 Squadron Lancaster piloted by F/O C. Burne. The aircraft crashes near Glinde, a small town east of Hamburg.

8. Beyond the immediate Hamburg area, the 156 Squadron aircraft of F/Sgt G.W. Wilkins is attacked by a nightfighter and he is blown out of the aircraft and survives to become a POW.

9. 02.30hrs: British bombers make for Wenzendorf and cross the German coast north of Bremerhaven. Here, route-markers, dropped near Spieka, give away the bombers' position and German night fighters enjoy success.

10. Day reconnaissance photographs show the huge damage caused to central and eastern Hamburg, particularly in the districts of Billwärder-Ausschlag, Grasbrook and St Georg.

5

Stade

9

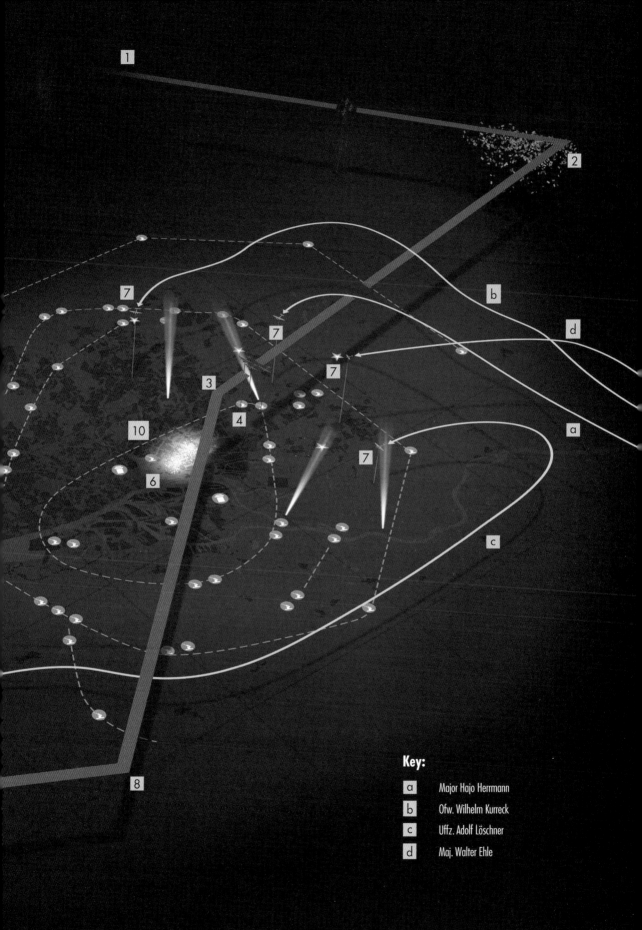

Key:

a   Major Hajo Herrmann

b   Ofw. Wilhelm Kurreck

c   Uffz. Adolf Löschner

d   Maj. Walter Ehle

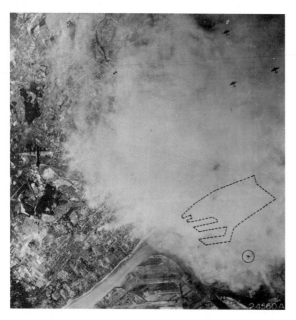

Lieutenant General Ira C. Eaker sent his bombers twice to Hamburg during Operation *Gomorrah*, which included this attack on the Blohm & Voss shipyards (its distinctive shape being drawn on the photograph). The Elbe and the Altona area can also be clearly seen. Against the smoke plume are B.17 Fortresses flying very low, whilst the aircraft circled is an Fw.190 day interceptor. (IWM FRE 4865)

83 Squadron recalled 'lightning struck our aircraft twice'; worse, while still approaching Hamburg, he observed what 'appeared to be lightning across the gap between two clouds' followed by an aircraft 'blow[ing] up in an orange and black ball of flame'. Thompson probably witnessed the explosion of the 103 Squadron Lancaster of Warrant Officer J.S. Stoneman, in which wreckage came down south of Harburg. For others, the flight became a desperate battle for survival as something very dangerous formed on their aircraft, namely icing. Near Heligoland, the port engine and airspeed indicator failed on Jack Currie's Lancaster, meaning maintaining the cruising altitude of 19,000ft became ever more challenging, in which every so often the aircraft jolted downwards several hundred feet. Near Hamburg, the real terror started when Currie manoeuvred into clouds to escape an exploding flak burst. '[W]ithin seconds the thirty-ton bomber was a toy for the storm to play with, the wheel locked, immobile as a rock [and] out of my control,' he described. 'I heard no engines only roaring wind and savage thunder-claps.' Currie's Lancaster was in a stall, spinning to port and going down at increasing speed. Only at 8,000ft, on the verge of telling his crew to jump, was some control regained, although the controls waggled loosely from left to right because, as the mid-upper gunner soon observed, the ailerons on both wings had snapped off. 'A few miles short of the target', the 103 Squadron Lancaster of Warrant Officer R.J. Bunten 'gave a convulsive shudder, turned over on to his port side and then fell clean out of the sky'. Only through quick thinking by the flight engineer in jettisoning the bomb load, 'feathering' the port engines whilst increasing power on the other side and helping his pilot wrestle the controls was normal flight resumed. Many aircrews just got somewhere near Hamburg, with 197 aircraft attacking alternative targets and 107 aborting, becoming angry in their post-operation interrogation about being forced to operate in such weather conditions. The raid report made the unintentionally wry comment that 'confusion caused by the Arctic conditions' meant locating where the sky markers fell and where the bombs dropped 'is impossible'.

The Battle of Hamburg was notable not just for destruction inflicted on the city, but also for the debut of Window. Paralysing the Kammhuber Line, the British listened to wireless traffic revealing the chaos sown amongst the defenders. Many night-fighter crews complained of being vectored on to 'too many hostiles' that promptly disappeared when located. Unteroffizier Otto Kutzner (V–NJG3), on his first operational flight on 24–25 July, recalled locating something, but it never was 'the slipstream of the bomber'. Peter Spoden (II–NJG-5), a rookie pilot based at Parchim, remembered patrolling box *Reiher* (Heron) near Lübeck and seeing the on-board Lichtenstein radar emitting 'flickering signals everywhere, but no readable echoes'. Soon becoming embroiled in a row with his ground controller, who wanted him to remain on station, as Spoden himself could see the bombers attacking Hamburg, he landed in a state of despair and exhaustion, and quickly found others had suffered the same experience. The rigidity of the Himmelbett patrol boxes was driving everyone mad amid the chaos and confusion now engulfing Germany's air defences. Devoid of 'eyes' to properly detect the bomber stream, night-fighter crews, searchlight personnel and flak gunners fought while never knowing where it truly was. Heavy flak defences put up intense barrages – to the continual consternation of the lower-flying Wellingtons and Stirlings – but its direction was largely based on guesswork. The searchlights, having had their range-finding radars jammed, wandered around erratically. Traugott Bauer-Schlichtegroll, a member of the 267th Heavy Flak Division, recalled that his gun crew quickly expended 160 rounds, but 'in the excitement of the battle, we did not notice that the command post was ordering the guns to fire in a completely wrong direction'.

Window's usage had paid dividends. Traditionally a costly target, Bomber Command lost just 12 bombers (1.5 per cent) when targeting Hamburg on 24–25 July, divided equally between flak and night fighters. Five came down near the target, the others around Heligoland, Cuxhaven or the Dutch coast. Two of 103 Squadron's three losses happened on the Dutch coast, with the Lancaster of Warrant Officer G.E.B. Hardman shot down by Hauptmann Rudolf Sigmund (IV–NJG1), the first British casualty of the Battle of Hamburg. The second Lancaster lost, piloted by Warrant Officer F.F. O'Hanlon, was attacked over the Frisian Islands by Sigmund's colleague, Oberleutnant Hermann Greiner. Years later, Greiner told Martin Middlebrook, author of *The Battle of Hamburg*:

> [O'Hanlon's Lancaster] was going so slowly that I overshot it on my first run. I soon saw the reason for this was that it had two engines failed, both on one side! It took me – for a combat situation – rather a long time to make up my mind what to do next… I didn't feel too happy about shooting him down though. However, I aimed, as in most other cases, very carefully at the wing tanks to give the crew a chance.

The second attack saw 2.2 per cent of the raiding force lost (17 aircraft), a small increase but well below the average loss rate for Hamburg operations before *Gomorrah* of 6.1 per cent. However, the post-raid assessment noted 'instances of aircraft held in searchlight cones but not engaged by flak'. This was because single-engined fighters were freelancing over the target area (*Wilde Sau*), using its brightness – be it the fires, target markers or searchlights – to locate an enemy aircraft. Not surprisingly, the bombers of the final waves, once Hamburg was well and truly alight, experienced greater combat. Major Hajo Herrmann shot down the 101 Squadron Lancaster of Flight Sergeant D.P.P. Hurst, which crashed into Wellingsbüttel, a northern district of Hamburg. For other night-fighter pilots, the night was about contradictory messages and sudden changes in information. Racing to Hamburg to find it 'blazing like a furnace', Wilhelm Johnen's ground controller then reported the bombers heading towards Heligoland. Johnen flew back to Venlo airfield in Holland, dejected at having drawn a blank.

Losses on the third attack increased to 28 aircraft (3.6 per cent), still a reasonable figure for this target but one that nonetheless continued the upward spike. The air defences remained hampered, but were detected to be stronger, both along the route and around Hamburg. An outer belt running from the north-east to the south-west was joined by an inner circle, which the British described as having the role of 'fighter guides'. Following the situation conference at the Führer's headquarters in Rastenburg on 28 July, Hitler – simultaneously dealing with crises in Russia (Kursk) and Italy (Mussolini's downfall) – made 'a violently critical

The Halifax V (427 Squadron) of Sgt R.L. Henry on the night of the Hamburg firestorm, 27–28 July 1943

This illustration depicts the aircraft of Sgt R.L. Henry which, owing to a late take-off, was the 731st and last aircraft to bomb the suffering city on that night at 01.47a.m., several minutes after the attack had officially finished. The 427 Squadron ORB records that Henry's aircraft drops its bomb load in the Hammerbrook area of the city, at the 'centre of conflagration as no T.I. markers visible due to smoke and haze'. It also notes the crew saw an 'enormous column of smoke and large concentration of fires all around target', indicative of the firestorm growing in its maximum intensity. A huge smoke column had risen up to 22,000ft by the time Henry's crew attacked the target, which was 2,000ft higher than the altitude of Henry's aircraft. By this time, the city's air-defences – as concentrated area-bombing fully intended – had collapsed. 'Defences fell away almost to nothing towards the end of the attack', the official report noted, which were also badly affected by Bomber Command's use of the Window countermeasure.

The remains of the 78 Squadron Mk.II Halifax piloted by Australian Flt Sgt P.A. Fraser. Hit by flak, probably when crossing the hot area around the Kiel Canal Zone, the aircraft crashed 12 miles S.W. of Lübeck. (IWM HU13165)

outburst against the Luftwaffe and demanded an immediate build-up in flak defences' in expectation of further attacks on Hamburg. Extra batteries were immediately sent, possibly including some of the 'emergency' railway-mounted ones. Flak downed six bombers over the city. Yet it was the *Wilde Sau*, together with twin-engined night fighters now operating in the target area, which left their mark. Many British aircrews reported becoming conned, flak being fired before promptly stopping, and then being attacked immediately by a night fighter. Forensic examination of the operation by the ORS (Operational Research Section) at HQ Bomber Command ascertained that 70 per cent of such encounters occurred between 17,000ft and 20,000ft. Oberleutnant Gerhard Rath (II–NJG-3) shot down a 77 Squadron Halifax and another from 158 Squadron, while Hauptmann Egmont Prinz zur Lippe-Weissenfeld (III–NJG1) downed the 460 (RAAF) Squadron Lancaster of Flying Officer A.J. Johnson. Oberleutnant Joachim Wendtland, the observer in Lippe-Weissenfeld's Bf.110, described how, initially patrolling their assigned box, they were finding the ground controller's contacts not genuine and were then instructed to freelance. Eventually locating Johnson's Lancaster 'clearly visible against the sky above us', they made the first of four attacks, hitting a wing and causing 'burning pieces' to fall off the aircraft. But the Lancaster kept going 'straight and level', not corkscrewing to evade the attacking night fighter, perhaps because the initial attack may have killed the air gunners or cut the intercom. Deploying 'his special method' of attack, Wendtland said Lippe-Weissenfeld:

> …slid under the bomber, pulled up the nose suddenly, fired a burst and dropped away quickly in case the bomber blew up. It didn't, although pieces were still falling off it. We attacked again. The bomber still didn't explode… We made one more attack and, this time, his wing started burning after only half a second. We saw the Lancaster go down into a wood near a railway.

The II–JG-300 *Wilde Sau* unit had another kill with Unteroffizier Harald Lövenich shooting down the Lancaster of Flight Sergeant H.L. Fuhrmann. Night fighters overall accounted for 11 aircraft and damaged another six; in return, the Luftwaffe had three aircraft destroyed in mid-air. The final attack revealed clearly that Window's effectiveness came when the bomber stream was compact, for in the prevailing weather conditions on this night it was not. Thirty aircraft were lost (4.0 per cent), many undoubtedly to icing, but stragglers were more easily found and picked off. Oberfeldwebel Karl-Heinz Scherfling (IV–NJG-1) destroyed a 9 Squadron Lancaster, Hauptmann Hans-Joachim Jabs (IV–NJG-1) downed one from 44 Squadron and a Stirling from 75 (NZ) Squadron, and two aircraft were claimed by Greiner.

Whilst Luftwaffe pilots bravely took on Bomber Command, Hitler himself consistently refused requests by Karl Kaufmann, the *Gauleiter* of Hamburg, and Speer to visit Hamburg, or meet rescue workers from it. The senior Nazi who did go was Göring, visiting on 6 August – decorating Hitler Youth flak gunners and addressing groups of civilians – before leaving promptly the next day. Goebbels also visited the city of his long-standing friend Kaufmann, and recorded in his diary that it represented a 'picture of the most appalling devastation'.

The British press called the outcome 'unparalleled in the history of air war'. Ultra decrypts (especially of Japanese diplomatic telegrams sent to Tokyo), accounts from seamen of neutral countries and reports in Swedish newspapers described Hamburg's plight in considerable –

and vivid – detail, information that was all analysed by experts in the MEW. Meanwhile, Admiral-of-the-Fleet, Sir Dudley Pound, the First Sea Lord, informed Harris the destruction caused was 'bound to have an effect on the Anti-U-boat war'. Replying, the Bomber Command C-in-C admitted:

> We have still, of course, quite a bit to do to Hamburg, and in the course of it hope to include further damage on the submarine yards. Nevertheless, I doubt if they will do much useful production for some time to come… From all reports, the entire place is in a state of chaos.

The 'chaos' was sufficient to ensure British heavy bombers would not return for a year. Six Mosquitoes made a harassing attack on 5–6 November and the US VIII Bomber Command attacked the city as an alternative target on 13 December 1943, but winter 1943–44 was the quietest part of the war for Hamburg's population. At Churchill's urging, and no doubt reading reports of widespread panic during summer 1943, Harris turned to Berlin. The level of destruction to Germany's second city nonetheless set the benchmark for Bomber Command's efforts elsewhere. To 'Hamburg' a city, as Bufton wrote about Leipzig on 18 October, became an adopted description.[6]

With Bomber Command's main strength deployed against other targets, attacks on Hamburg during the first part of 1944 were restricted to Mosquito raids. The city did endure heavy attacks, but these were American ones that targeted its refineries in the campaign against Germany's oil that began on 12 May. The US Eighth Air Force first attacked Hamburg on 18 June, but the 522 Fortresses of 1BD (1st Bomb Division) and 421 Liberators of 2BD (2nd Bomb Division) missed their assigned targets. German historian Jörg Friedrich points out that whilst the firestorm had devastated the working-class areas of eastern Hamburg, it 'barely touched the historic center of the city'; instead, the Americans would do so on this attack. 'A few seconds' delay' in releasing the bombs on Harburg's oil refineries 'shifted the impact to very different targets', ones of 'no interest' such as St James's Church. The US Eighth returned consistently to the city's oil refineries, attacking on 20 June, 4 and 6 August, 6 and 25 October and 4 and 6 November. Post-raid assessments revealed the Americans were hitting their targets, often leaving devastation and fierce fires around the refineries and storage tanks.

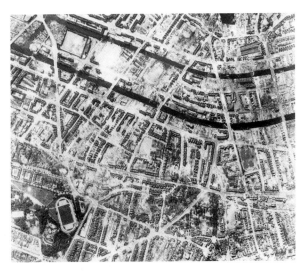

The vastness of Hamburg's destruction during Operation *Gomorrah* can be seen in this aerial reconnaissance photograph, in which the 1,000 °C fires had raged through the central and eastern districts. A colossal total of 26,200 H.E.'s and 3,085,500 I.B.'s were dropped. Central Hamburg was divided into three zones: a 'dead-zone', completely destroyed and declared off-limits; an 'evacuated zone' where public utilities were destroyed and entry was only by special permits; and a 'live zone', which had partial destruction but was undergoing gradual repair. (Getty Images)

Bomber Command's 'anniversary' raid

On 28–29 July 1944, perhaps with the events of 12 months before in mind, Harris mounted a major attack on Hamburg simultaneously with the third night in a concentrated series of raids, 'Hamburg-style', against another city, Stuttgart. Possibly stung by Churchill's assertion that 'the flying-bombs caused 8 to 10 times the damage caused by a comparable weight of our bombs', the C-in-C set out to prove his case about Bomber Command's destructiveness by returning to the bombing of Germany's cities. A sky-marking effort, the Hamburg raid began at 0110hrs (the Stuttgart attack commencing 35 minutes later), resulting in

---

6   On 19 October, the Defence Committee ruled the 'best method of bringing the Bulgars to heel' was bombing Sofia after dropping leaflets, 'citing [the] fate of Hamburg'.

Joseph Goebbels, Reichsminister of Public Enlightenment and Propaganda, and diarist. On 29 July, right before the third attack, he wrote 'Kaufmann, in a first report, spoke of a catastrophe the extent of which simply staggers the imagination. A city of a million inhabitants has been destroyed in a manner unparalleled in history. We are faced with problems that are almost impossible of solution . . . He spoke of about 800,000 homeless people wandering up and down the streets not knowing what to do'. (Getty Images)

scattered bombing falling on areas most affected by the *Gomorrah* attacks. This killed 265 people and forced the evacuation of 17,000 inhabitants because a considerable proportion of temporary wooden houses had been hit. Once again, de-housing people had been Bomber Command's intended aim – and the result. Nonetheless, the cost to Bomber Command was high. Sixty-two aircraft failed to return, with 7.2 per cent (22 aircraft) losses to the Hamburg force and 7.9 per cent (39 aircraft) to the Stuttgart one. The 7–9–/10ths cloud provided no cover above 10,000ft, and in the clear sky 300 night fighters were operating. Two-thirds of these operated against the Stuttgart force on its outward journey. This was the opposite experience of the Hamburg force, which was engaged by a considerable number of night fighters on the homebound journey from the Schleswig coastline to Heligoland; losses solely from 6 Group were 13 Halifaxes (five coming from 431 Squadron) and four Lancasters missing. An investigation launched by Air Vice-Marshal C.M. McEwen found some aircraft leaving Hamburg stayed above the thick cloud in bright skies for too long. In such conditions, the night fighters had 'an unusually favourable opportunity, which was exploited vigorously and with considerable success'. The night's losses caused gloomy conclusions to emerge about the battle between British countermeasures and German night fighters, and Harris told Sir Arthur Street, Permanent Secretary at the Air Ministry, the latter's rejuvenation meant Bomber Command's mission would become 'considerably more severe'. In many ways, this represented over-worry. The light night and huge numbers of night fighters in western Germany had allowed an exceptionally good result. From mid-August, Bomber Command had exceptionally low losses; raids on Stettin and Kiel saw just ten aircraft lost from 806 bombers sent (1.24 per cent), whilst 288 aircraft attacking Bremen suffered only one Lancaster missing.

During August, raids on Hamburg were small-scale efforts. On 18–19 August, three very rare Mk VI Lancasters (these having upgraded Merlin engines) from 635 Squadron were sent to bomb the Preussische-Elektrizitätswerke power station in Harburg. One dropped its bombs, another aborted and the third aircraft of Flight Sergeant P. Robinson was coned and despatched by flak over the target. Nine Mosquito attacks continued, becoming heavier, between 6–7 September and 11–12 December. Just two Mosquitoes were lost from all these attacks.

Oil and U-boats, September 1944–April 1945

In late September 1944, Harris was finally released from SHAEF's (Supreme Headquarters Allied Expeditionary Force) control. 'We should now get on and knock Germany flat,' Harris told Churchill. Yet the C-in-C would not regain the wide latitude over target policy he previously enjoyed. On 5 October 1944, the Combined Strategic Targets Committee (CSTC) was established to advise the new overlords of the Anglo-American bombing campaign in Europe, namely Deputy CAS Norman Bottomley and Lieutenant General Carl Spaatz (commander of Strategic Air Forces in Europe), on target priorities. The CSTC consistently championed attacking Germany's oil, and on 19 October sent Harris a target list headed by the plants at Leuna and Pölitz, with oil refineries in Harburg next.

Telling him that resumption of activity at any of these plants would 'add significantly to the enemy's supplies of motor and aviation gasoline', the particular importance of the Harburg refineries was their ability to refine Hungarian crude, and the JIC wanted them attacked immediately. On 1 November, a directive was given to both strategic air forces ordering the destruction of Germany's oil refineries. This began the long, bitter 'oil vs cities' debate between Portal and Harris throughout winter 1944–45, conducted in 12 often-lengthy letters. The crux of the divergence is encapsulated by Portal's comment on 12 November that 'if I knew you [Harris] to be as wholehearted in the attack of oil as in the past you have been in the matter of attacking cities I would have little to worry about'. But Harris maintained his view. In an unintentionally amusing comment, on 29 December he wrote that 'we must be careful not to give the Germans the idea that by merely blowing out a jet or two of steam they can egg us on into unnecessary attacks [on oil refineries]'.

Ironically, Portal's earlier criticism was written the day after Harris *had* bombed oil refineries at Harburg, Dortmund and Kamen. A force of 237 Lancasters and eight Mosquitoes – all from 5 Group, which throughout 1944 frequently operated as a quasi-

The American raid on 20 June 1944. The distinctive shape of the Elbe and Hamburg's docks, with American bombers attacking the refineries at Harburg, south of the river, can be clearly seen. (Getty Images)

independent force within Bomber Command – dropped 920 tons of bombs on Harburg's oil plants to back up the two American attacks made over the previous week. Conducted in fine weather, closer inspection reveals the Command's old views on targeting still remained. The ORB of 460 (RAAF) Squadron reveals there were three aiming points: two over the Ebano and Rhenania oil refineries for aircraft carrying large HE loads and one over Harburg's town centre for aircraft packed with incendiaries. An H2S-assisted Newhaven attack saw bombing initially scattered, but it soon became concentrated. Explosions were seen, including a huge one at 1928hrs, and fires blazed away at the oil targets. As for the town, 467 Squadron crews reported this as being 'well alight' by the end. Daylight photography revealed an 80ft storage tank at the Ebano refinery had been consumed by fire, and the surrounding port, its quaysides, cranes, warehouses and marshalling yard had all suffered damage; houses and shops had been destroyed in the northern part of the town. Over Harburg, air bomber Sergeant John Aldridge (49 Squadron) remembered 'the flak was very, very thick that night' and 'approaching the target there was just above me … one great explosion'. Observing 'pieces falling down', this was most likely the Lancaster of Aldridge's commanding officer, Squadron Leader H. Gorton, with most of the wreckage landing in Wilhelmsburg. Another aircraft was also downed by flak, two from a mid-air collision and a further three shot down by night fighters, thus the 2.8 per cent loss rate was much lower than expected for a vital oil target. This low tally came despite the Harburg force being plotted early and night fighters waiting over Heligoland and Hamburg. Yet German controllers also tracked the Dortmund force and mistakenly concluded the Harburg one was a spoof attack, thereby ordering many night fighters to fly towards the Ruhr.

There were no more heavy attacks on Hamburg by Bomber Command in 1944, indeed none until 5 Group's effort on 21–22 March 1945. The US Eighth attacked Hamburg's oil refineries on 31 December. Following the Elbe to the specific targets, one American airman remembered 'the flak was brutal', with the Fortresses flying through thick explosions and having pieces shot off the aircraft 'for what seemed like an hour'. Upon leaving Hamburg, German day fighters made their move against the bombers, which now flew into a strong headwind. Twenty-seven aircraft were listed as missing and an eye-watering 288 returned damaged.

Beyond its oil industry, Hamburg was retargeted because of the new models of U-boat Dönitz wanted

Notwithstanding the commitment to precision-bombing, American bombs did not always fall where intended. This photograph, taken after the 18 June 1944 attack that marked the start of the consistent American attack on Hamburg's oil targets, shows some having partially demolished a large company building in the city area several miles from the oil refineries south of the river. (Getty Images)

OPPOSITE THE DUAL ATTACK ON HARBURG AND DORTMUND'S OIL REFINERIES, 11–12 NOVEMBER 1944

for restarting the campaign in the Atlantic. With prefabricated construction drastically reducing building time from 11 months to four, in October 1944 the MEW assessed that output would soon equate to the former peak level of production in mid-1943, which meant about 500 U-boats would be operational by February 1945. Increasingly alarmed, once again the Admiralty wanted Bomber Command's assistance against the building yards. Yet the Air Staff pointed out that experience from 1943, when a substantial effort was made against these targets, had yielded 'only a marginal effect on the production of submarines'. For this reason, Bufton wrote on 17 October that 'we should strongly resist any undertaking to divert effort to these targets'. Bombing U-boat production was perceived as yielding results only in the long term, unlike attacking oil that in the short term promised the greatest dividend of all, namely Germany's capitulation. Attacking oil, moreover, threatened the diesel fuel needed by U-boats – the MEW assessing 16,000 tons being required every month for training, working-up and operations – and offered 'a far better prospect of preventing the large increase in the operational activity of U-boats anticipated by the Admiralty'. However, photographic reconnaissance taken in January 1945 of Hamburg, Bremen and Kiel revealed 48 Type XXIs and 26 Type XXIIIs had been completed, with many more being laid down. Consequently, the Combined Chiefs of Staff concluded this represented a serious threat to the shipping lanes around Britain, and on 7 February ordered that, after oil and transportation, marginal bombing effort was to be used against building yards, 'concentrating on Hamburg and Bremen'.

Major attacks by Bomber Command and the Eighth Air Force against Hamburg in 1945 (* = use of special rocket-assisted 4,500lb bomb called 'Disney')				
Target(s) in Hamburg	Date	Air Force	Despatched	Tons dropped
Rhenania-Ossag Mineralölwerke (Grasbrook) Rhenania-Ossag Mineralölwerke (Harburg) Blohm & Voss	17 January	US	242	617.2
Rhenania-Ossag Mineralölwerke (Harburg) Ebano Asphaltwerke (Harburg) Deutsche Erdölwerke (Wilhelmsburg)	24 February	US	362	1,014
Rhenania-Ossag Mineralölwerke (Harburg)	5 March	US	126	323.5
Rhenania-Ossag Mineralölwerke (Harburg)	7–8 March	RAF	241	1,107
Blohm & Voss	8–9 March	RAF	312	945
Rhenania-Ossag (Grasbrook)	11 March	US	485	1,123.8
Deutsche-Erdölwerke (Wilhelmsburg) Blohm & Voss Port area	20 March	US	314	867.4
Deutsche Erdölwerke (Wilhelmsburg)	21–22 March	RAF	159	441
Blohm & Voss Deutsche Werft (Finkenwärder) Port area Oil depot	30 March	US	530	1,398.5
Blohm & Voss	31 March	RAF	469	2,503
Deutsche Werft (Finkenwärder)	4 April	US	24	99*
Rhenania-Ossag Mineralölwerke (Harburg)	4–5 April	RAF	327	1,430
Blohm & Voss	8–9 April	RAF	440	1,683
U-boat pens (Finkenwärder) Europäische Tanklager (Petroleum-Hafen)	9 April	RAF	59	106

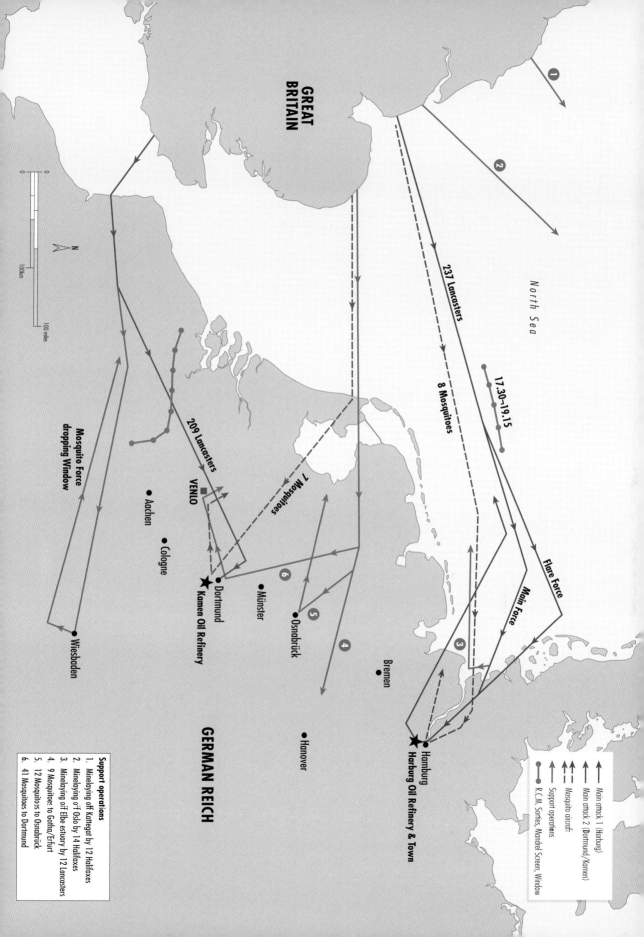

GREAT BRITAIN

North Sea

GERMAN REICH

237 Lancasters

17.30–19.15

8 Mosquitoes

Flare Force

Main Force

209 Lancasters

7 Mosquitoes

VENLO

Mosquito Force dropping Window

Aachen

Cologne

Dortmund
★ Kamen Oil Refinery

Münster

Osnabrück

Bremen

Hanover

Wiesbaden

Hamburg
★ Harburg Oil Refinery & Town

0
100km
0
100 miles

N

1
2
3
4
5
6

Support operations
1. Minelaying off Kattegat by 12 Halifaxes
2. Minelaying of Oslo by 14 Halifaxes
3. Minelaying off Elbe estuary by 12 Lancasters
4. 9 Mosquitoes to Gotha/Erfurt
5. 12 Mosquitoes to Osnabrück
6. 41 Mosquitoes to Dortmund

Main attack 1 (Harburg)
Main attack 2 (Dortmund/Kamen)
Mosquito aircraft
Support operations
R.C.M. Sorties, Mandrel Screen, Window

Admiral Andrew Cunningham, who became the First Sea Lord by 1944–45 and one of the Chiefs of Staff alongside Portal and Field-Marshal Alan Brooke, continually pressed for Bomber Command's assistance against the threat from new types of U-Boat. He was no admirer of Harris; his diary entry for 16 June 1942 described meeting 'the bomber king whom I cordially disliked'. (Getty Images)

Bomber Command's raids against Hamburg resumed on 7–8 March, although to the Admiralty's disappointment the targets were Harburg's oil refineries. Reconnaissance on 24 February showed these plants had been repaired and were about to resume production. Seven Mosquitoes and 234 Lancasters were sent by 5 Group to knock out the plants, with the bombing done from around 11,000ft. Even this late on, attacking an oil target represented a perilous prospect, as wireless operator Warrant Officer J. Shearing (49 Squadron) described:

When we started our bombing run all hell started up; we bombed and 20 seconds later we were hit by flak – the whole kite shuddered. The run out of the target was a nightmare, we saw five confirmed Lancs go down, one which a parachute came out of – saw several other kites that were probables. The flak was deadly, mostly light stuff sent up in a hosepipe form and fighters all around.

Fourteen Lancasters (6.0 per cent) were lost, a high casualty figure by this stage of the war, with four from 189 Squadron alone, which showed the Germans continued to defend their vital targets viciously. Early plotting of the Harburg force allowed four Gruppen to take off. Sent initially to Kiel, the mistake was corrected and the Luftwaffe caught the bombers on their final run into the target. Fifteen combats took place there, six over Harburg and another two over the Weser estuary. Night fighters shot down nine Lancasters (64.3 per cent of those lost), flak another three, and the fate of the remaining two was unknown. With other operations, 1,269 aircraft were involved in raids on this night and a total of 41 (3.2 per cent) were lost – casualties Harris' gigantic bomber force could nonetheless absorb.

The bombs of 5 Group found their mark, the plants quickly becoming engulfed by large explosions and vast fires emitting thick black smoke plumes up to 10,000ft. Reconnaissance on 8 March revealed destruction to cracking installations, storage tanks and pipelines, and little activity remaining. The 1,107 tons of bombs dropped to knock out Harburg's plants capped a week in which Bomber Command had released 7,300 tons on oil refineries throughout Germany, alongside the major efforts of the US Eighth. This intense effort, the CSTC reported, was designed 'to exert a decisive influence upon the operational capabilities of all branches of the German Armed Forces in the critical phase of the Battle of Germany'.

The following night, whilst a large force of 37 Halifaxes and 27 Lancasters mined the Elbe and Weser to stop U-boats from entering the North Sea, 4, 6 and 8 Groups sent 241 Halifaxes, 62 Lancasters and nine Mosquitoes against the Blohm & Voss shipyards. Initially a ground marking effort, cloud forced the switch to sky marking, the bombs falling south-west of the shipyard and no damage being done to the U-boat assembly slips. In contrast to the stiff defences encountered in the previous attack, night fighters shot down just one aircraft – the 415 (RCAF) Squadron Halifax piloted by Warrant Officer I.A.F. McDiarmid – and only one more air combat occurred. Hamburg's flak and searchlights were less effective, perhaps because of the cloud, but also due to ammunition for the 88mm guns being increasingly short. On 2 March, an Ultra decrypt revealed flak batteries had been ordered to fire only when presented with an exceptional chance of downing an Allied bomber.

From 21–22 March to 13–14 April, a period of just over three weeks, Hamburg endured its final onslaught: three heavy night attacks, two daylight attacks and five Mosquito raids. The first, on 21–22 March, saw 5 Group return to attack an oil refinery, destroying the distillation plant, buildings of the fuel-processing section, 20 storage tanks and adjacent railway sidings. The refinery was inactive when captured by the British Army in May. Three Lancasters were lost to flak and another was shot down by a night fighter.

Following Mosquito raids on 29–30 March and the following night, Bomber Command's next heavy attack would be in daylight on 31 March. Some weeks before, Hitler, having made 'the most violent criticism of Göring' and describing the Luftwaffe as 'a great junk shop', declared only the Me.262 offered 'some great hope' for daytime defence. British intelligence detected that night fighter units were being told to relinquish pilots for emergency training on the Me.262. Meanwhile, autobahns were being prepared as potential runways, with concealed dispersal points placed in wooded areas. On 27 March, the former head of the V-weapons programme, SS-General Hans Kammler, was placed in charge of the jet production programme, while Generalmajor Dietrich Peltz was assigned to orchestrate Me.262 daylight operations and the rehabilitated Kammhuber for their night-time role, all too little too late.

On 30 March, some 20 Me.262s opposed the US Eighth's attack on Hamburg and Bremen, and therefore were already in the vicinity for aggressive attacks on Bomber Command's effort the following day. Escorted by 12 squadrons of Mustangs, 469 heavy bombers were sent to administer the *coup de grâce* to the Blohm & Voss shipyards, but damaging them only slightly, they encountered Germany's jet fighters for the first time. Upon sighting one, operational procedure called for bombers to fire off red and green rounds from their Very flare pistols to alert the fighter escorts. Compared to the Americans, however, the British were novices when it came to organizing escorted operations in daylight. On this occasion, the final wave of 100 Lancasters from 6 Group was late and the Mustangs, assuming the bomber stream was complete, proceeded without it. The initial two waves were attacked by a few Me.262s – 7 Squadron flight engineer Warrant Officer Harold Lazenby observing 'it was a rough-looking aircraft with no paint nor markings' – but the unescorted group encountered many more over Hamburg. Based at Parchim, expert pilots from III–JG-7 tore into the formation. With lethal, aircraft-shredding heavy cannons, the ferocity of the Me.262's rapier-like attacks was intense. Flying Officer K.K. Blyth, a pilot with 408 (RCAF) Squadron, recalled:

The tail gunner later reported he had seen a spot on the turret Perspex and the next thing an Me262 came out of the sun and we had been hit. Its 30-mm. cannon shell blew off two of the guns on the tail turret and bent another. The cone of fire centred on the port wing and port outer engine. We were on fire and totally out of control.

Hamburg's female tram-drivers in September 1944. Women in all countries during the war undertook many tasks hitherto reserved for men. Female employment, of course, ran counter to traditional Nazi ideology but the demands of Total War by 1944 meant dogma had to be pushed to one side. For all cities, local transportation was vital for workers travelling to factories and shipyards, thereby continuing essential war production. (Getty Images)

5 Group's daylight attack on Hamburg, 9 April 1945

On 9 April 1945, 57 Lancasters from 5 Group, including 17 aircraft from the Dambusters unit (617 Squadron), executed a daylight operation against the reinforced concrete U-Boat pens at Finkenwärder and the nearby oil-storage tanks at Petroleum Hafen. With two aircraft dropping what 617 Squadron's ORB described as the 'special store', namely the 22,000ib Grand Slam bomb, and other Lancasters releasing the 12,000ib 'Tallboy', this illustration depicts the raid from Harburg looking north towards the south bank of the Elbe where the two targets were situated. Several bombs have hit the U-Boat pens, which caused erupting large fireballs, whilst the following Lancasters fly in a gaggle formation between 10–13,000ft. Under attack from an Me.262 jet fighter, one of a dozen roaring around the target area, and enduring the heavy flak still defending this area of Hamburg, the 50 Squadron Lancaster hit was piloted by Australian Flying Officer V.G. Berriman, whose objective was the oil-storage tanks, and who crashed in the target area.

The M.E.W.'s final report on Hamburg stated 'in the full built-up area the destruction and damage to property amounts to over 77 per cent [some ten sq. miles] . . . In all 1,220 acres of business and residential property in the fully built-up town area have been completely destroyed, and another 864 acres in the outer areas'. (Getty Images)

The aircraft crashed into the Bergedorf district, the crew escaping to become late-war POWs, one of three Halifaxes that – together with eight Lancasters – comprised Bomber Command's last double-digit loss of the war.

On 4–5 April, 14 Pathfinder Mosquitoes led 277 Halifaxes and 36 Lancasters from 4 and 6 Groups against the Rhenania-Ossag plant in Harburg, 'the intention' being 'to complete destruction of [the] repaired and partly active [installation]'. Assisted by Mosquito spoof raids, intruder patrols and 136 aircraft from 100 Group making RCM sorties (its largest of the war), these support operations clearly worked, for although five night-fighter Gruppen operated that night, only one Halifax was shot down (flak accounting for two Lancasters). Many night fighters, informed that the Harburg force was a feint, only realized the error once the bombers were heading back towards the Zuider Zee. By this time, the refinery was a blazing wreck; 1,430 tons of bombs severely damaged the distillation unit and two boiler houses, whilst ten storage tanks were gutted by fire. Four nights later, Bomber Command switched its attention back to Hamburg's shipyards and port area, which contained large concentrations of merchant shipping. The 2,503 tons dropped by 440 heavy bombers caused severe damage to Blohm & Voss, Stülcken and Howaldtswerke. Five Gruppen of night fighters once again initially missed the Hamburg force because of being ordered to intercept the feint attack on Travemünde by 22 Halifaxes. Three groups turned to Hamburg once the actual target became clear, but by then were committed to a stern chase. The bombers' sudden directional change and rapid loss of height shook off the pursuers, and just three Lancasters and three Halifaxes were lost.

Daylight on 9 April saw large numbers of Mustangs and Spitfires escort 59 5 Group Lancasters, which included 17 aircraft from 617 Squadron. All carried Bomber Command's large 'special bombs', namely Grand Slams and Tallboys, to be dropped on the concrete U-boat pens at Finkenwärder. Five crashed through the thick roof (leaving hourglass-shaped holes ranging from 14–25ft in diameter), another detonated within 100ft – causing damage to a lateral supporting wall – three landed between 130ft and 300ft away and two fell into the Elbe. However, the USSBS found 'damage from these hits was not serious'; the roof holes were repaired by 'reinforced concrete plugs' and only minor damage was caused to cranes and switchboards inside the pens. Simultaneously, Petroleum-Hafen was attacked by another 40 Lancasters, whose Tallboys knocked out the refinery's distillation unit, popped 23 storage tanks and significantly damaged the loading jetties. Me.262s shot down two Lancasters over Hamburg.

The citizens of Hamburg never experienced another attack by four-engine British bombers, but the Mosquitoes still came to administer their 'sting'. Twenty-four of them made a diversionary attack on 9–10 April in support of a huge raid on Kiel aiming to destroy large concentrations of Type XXI U-boats and the remnants of Germany's surface battle fleet. Four nights later, a particularly large effort by 87 Mosquitoes made against the Blohm & Voss shipyards saw the final 106 tons of bombs dropped on Hamburg. Within days, a new directive issued to the strategic bomber forces terminated the bombing offensive. The aim of the 'progressive destruction and dislocation of the German military, industrial and economic systems' had been achieved. Hamburg's dreadful ordeal from aerial bombardment was over.

AFTERMATH AND ANALYSIS

'[T]error attacks … do us considerably more harm than attacks on purely industrial installations, as the loss of workers and working hours is incalculable'

German Air Ministry Memorandum, 27 November 1943

'It is remarkable how Hamburg … was back to 80% of normal production within 5 months [of *Gomorrah*]'

Air Commodore Sydney Bufton, August 1945

Operation *Gomorrah* saw 3,000 sorties and 8,500 tons of bombs dropped on the city of Hamburg, destroying 6,200 from 8,382 acres of the city's built-up area (74 per cent) and becoming, in Arthur Harris' words, 'a scene of unimaginable devastation'. In comparison, central London suffered 600 acres of destruction during the Blitz, and Coventry, the city whose attack represented an important milestone in the development of British bombing policy, a mere 135 acres. Hamburg had 35,719 of 58,476 buildings totally destroyed, and 4,685 severely damaged, with 24 hospitals, 58 churches, 277 schools, vast numbers of warehouses, 186 large factories and 4,118 small firms completely wrecked. Some 180,000 tons of shipping was sunk in the docks. The ORS at HQ Bomber Command calculated that 61 per cent of dwellings in the city were levelled. Attacks by Bomber Command either side of *Gomorrah*, and raids by the US Eighth, contributed 1,200 acres of additional destruction, making the total area destroyed in Hamburg 7,400 acres, which represented 16 per cent of the total urban devastation inflicted by Allied bombers on Germany during World War II. The second city was the third most-devastated German city, behind gutted Remscheid and Kassel.

A total of 900,000 people were rendered de-housed, between 800,000 and 1.1 million evacuated and anywhere from 30,000–50,000 (figures greatly vary) killed in the 'firestorm' attack alone. Precise figures were difficult to ascertain because intense fires left piles of ash

in basements and small air raid shelters, making it impossible to determine how many human beings had originally been there. The Reich Statistics Office put the 'firestorm' deaths figure at 41,450, but rounded this up later to 42,600 to include the missing (broken down into 50 per cent women, 38 per cent men and 12 per cent children), equating to 80 per cent of Britain's dead during the entire Blitz. Illustrating the human carnage from the 27–28 July attack was that only 494 were killed in 15 raids during 1941, and 626 in 42 raids the following year. The two American attacks in July 1943 killed 440 people, while two raids by the US Eighth in October 1944 killed another 641. About 55,000 people died in Hamburg because of aerial bombing, the overwhelming majority coming from the one attack by Bomber Command. Because of this, the RAF's *Terrorflieger* were hated; the Americans, in contrast, were perceived 'as soldiers' because they attacked military targets 'during the daytime … and risked the aimed fire of our Flak'. '[We had] a certain respect for the "Amis" as we called them', one Hamburg civilian remembered.

Hamburg had 22,583 tons of bombs dropped by Bomber Command from 1940–45, and 15,736 tons of bombs by the USAAF. Although not as high as Berlin (45,517 tons by Bomber Command and 22,768 by the USAAF) and Cologne (34,712 and 13,302 tons, respectively) the extensive destruction to Hamburg can be clearly seen from this overhead view, a sight that would have greeted the small party from the Air Ministry, including Bufton, when they flew over the city in June 1945. (Getty Images)

Eyewitness accounts from Hamburg make for horrific, even moving, reading. Police officer Otto Müller described collecting incendiary-burnt victims, with a doctor making a quick choice between those who might survive and those who would not. In Wandsbek, he witnessed a young girl dragging her dead little brother, causing the right side of his face to be 'scraped smooth'. Others were seen sinking into melted asphalt or desperately scrambling onto a train. In one instance, 'a half-crazed woman' dropped her suitcase that sprang open 'to reveal clothes, a toy and the shrivelled, carbonized body of a child'. Survivors recalled the unforgettable 'howl' of the firestorm raging outside the air raid shelters, the desperate cries of latecomers trying to get in and the equally desperate cries of people mentally cracking up inside them. German historian Jörg Friedrich pertinently observes: 'Department stores burned best of all; they went up like torches, quickly igniting the wider surroundings. No cellar could withstand the heat of a glowing, red-hot department store, such as the Karstadt store in the Barmbek district of Hamburg.' Former Chancellor of West Germany Helmut Schmidt, whose parents lived in the area and perished alongside many other relatives, understandably always maintained 'it was wholly unjustified, indeed it was inexcusable'.

In 1947, Harris rationalized the raids by writing that the Luftwaffe had taught everybody the value of mass incendiary bombing, starting with Coventry. Had it 'gone on using the same force for several nights', he wrote, 'the whole of London would have gone as Hamburg went'. Such was military logic at its coldest, which sits uncomfortably with the morals and mores of the modern world, should one feel the need to judge the former by the latter. Some have done so, such as A.C. Grayling. Yet Tami Biddle is perfectly correct in commenting that Grayling's work, *Among the Dead Cities*, 'sought to apply 21st century moral and legal standards to a mid-twentieth century event', which can only carry an analysis so far.

On 3 May 1995, the 50th anniversary of Hamburg's surrender, King Charles III (then Prince of Wales) laid wreaths at Ohlsdorf Cemetery. Opened in August 1952 on the site of mass graves for many of the city's dead, this was a fitting act of reconciliation prior to the new century. Yet Israeli historian Gilad Margalit observes that the 60th anniversary remembrance of *Gomorrah* in July 2003 meant:

certain voices in the political culture of the Federal Republic echoed Jörg Friedrich's rage at the Allied conduct of strategic bombing in his books *Der Brand* and *Brandstätten* ... [with the] insinuated reference to the Allied bombing as a sort of a 'German Holocaust' (i.e. by calling a British squadron an *Einsatzgruppe* [the name given to the SS death squads]).

Ironically, German wartime opinion saw British area bombing quite differently. In April 1944, the *Reichsluftfahrtministerium* produced a paper stating that the 'terror attacks' were:

[of] thoroughly practical importance as a method of attacking the war economy, as it is easier to put one-third of the working capacity out of action by destroying homes and disrupting transport and supply services than to destroy one-third of all the factories. Moreover, being an area bombing attack, the terror attack on residential districts offers greater prospects of success than the pin-point attack on industrial plants. In these circumstances the maximum effect on the war economy is promised by large-scale area attacks on cities... Terror attacks [in] which use is made of incendiaries on densely populated cities, i.e. with closely built dwellings of several storeys, have proved to be particularly effective... [By] large-scale area attacks on cities ... the enemy has found a means of attacking the war economy.

As ghastly as area bombing undoubtedly was, a key question remains: was it successful in affecting war production in Hamburg?

Top priority under the Battle of the Atlantic Directive of March 1941, bombing scarcely affected submarine production during the early part of the war, and attacks of 1942 and early 1943 similarly did little. But using estimates, Webster and Frankland calculated the nine months *after* July 1943 saw production of 27 U-boats lost. The USSBS concluded that Allied attacks on Hamburg in July 1943, December 1944 and January–April 1945 accounted for 54 U-boats of various models. In summer 1945, they visited the Blohm & Voss and Howaldtswerke shipyards, saying these targets allowed for 'a comparison between the effects of area bombing and of precision bombing'. Observing the British raids of summer 1943 'had no material effect on [U-boat] production', they also stated that neither did the American precision raids of August–December 1944. Instead, the USSBS focused on the effect of British and American bombing methods on labour. Area bombing, they

The horrific faces of destruction: two charred corpses lie in front of a destroyed building (left) whilst a group of children lie dead having been asphyxiated during the firestorm on 27–28 July 1943. The suffering for Hamburg's civilian population was terrible; probably around 41,800 dead and 37,439 injured, and many more simply remaining missing. 'No flight of imagination', the Police President of Hamburg wrote, 'will ever succeed in measuring and describing the gruesome scenes of horror in the many buried air raid shelters . . . sacrificed by the murderous lust of a sadistic enemy'. (Getty Image)

acknowledged, made absenteeism longer in duration than that caused by precision attacks, which saw workers take shelter rather than abandon the city altogether. Nonetheless, for both strategic bomber forces, the on-site investigations revealed just how difficult a shipyard was to destroy, a facility where many bombs either impacted on concrete quaysides or fell harmlessly into water. Karl-Otto Saur, Speer's deputy, stated: that 'there was actually little direct damage' to building yards until the spring 1945 attacks, when it became serious 'with the destruction of floating cranes'. As Speer told British investigators, bombing building yards caused production losses of just 10 per cent, with damaged or partially sunk U-boats often raised and repaired. The key to affecting U-boat production, he added, was bombing towns making specialist components, particularly accumulator batteries, electric motors and diesel engines, which all represented severe bottlenecks. Later on, breaching the Dortmund–Ems Canal interrupted transportation of prefabricated hull sections made in Essen and Krefeld to the assembly yards at Hamburg and Bremen. The USSBS noted that the sections passing through the Münster locks in September 1944 numbered 107 before falling to 30, 18 and 17 over the following three months. Like other war industries, dispersed production became vulnerable once the Allies made concentrated attacks on Germany's transportation system from autumn 1944. Bombing Germany's railway system, especially in and around the Ruhr, also disrupted coal supplies, affecting Hamburg's power stations and causing governor Karl Kaufmann to declare a state of emergency in the city. Examination of the city's factories and interrogation of their owners revealed to American investigators that choking off coal supplies and other raw materials was vital in finishing off Hamburg's war industries and merchant shipping fleet. The BBSU (British Bombing Survey Unit), headed by Professor Solly Zuckerman, came to a similar conclusion. '[T]he crucial blow inflicted to Hamburg's economy', he wrote, was 'the transportation difficulties that resulted from air raids against railroad and canal installations'.

What, then, was the effect of bombing Hamburg's oil refineries? Examining the plants and tank farms throughout summer 1945, the USSBS stated that 'precision attacks caused a production loss approximately three times as great as that resulting from area raids'. Generally, however, the trend was initial and regular damage inflicted by the US Eighth being capped by Bomber Command inflicting the *coup de grâce* on these plants in spring 1945. Thus, a combined effort ensured Hamburg's oil refineries barely functioned, with American persistence complemented by British destructiveness. The Rhenania-Ossag Mineralölwerke at Wilhelmsburg illustrates the point. Just four attacks caused 60 per cent damage to the refinery, with the processing facilities and storage tanks particularly damaged by the US Eighth on 20 June 1944, but it was Bomber Command's attack on 21–22 March 1945 which destroyed the distillation unit, causing production to cease. Similarly, the Europäische-Tanklager AG storage facility suffered six attacks, but the last one on 9 April, when Bomber Command's Tallboy 'popped' many of the giant storage tanks, caused thousands of tons of finished, semi-finished and crude products to be lost.

Hamburg's giant port and merchant fleet were hardly affected by the bombing during the early years, but this changed with the *Katastrophe* of summer 1943. However, the British were only too aware of how quickly Hamburg recovered. Using photographic reconnaissance, the MEW observed that what had been a 'dead' port in mid-August recovered sufficiently some weeks later to handle the ships carrying vital iron ore

Dwellings amongst a ruined city; Hamburg's population in temporary shelters on the rubble-cleared streets in late 1945. (Getty Images)

from Sweden. '[T]he expectations of the Germans that they would be able to get the port working to 70% of its previous activity by the end of August,' the MEW noted, 'have largely been realised.' Physically eliminating the port area was impossible owing to its miles of quaysides; instead, what restricted shipping was continually absent dockworkers.

Ultimately, one way or another, British bombing policy was about making sure industrial workers were unable to produce in Germany's war factories. How this actually occurred did not matter so long as workplace absenteeism was the result, whether through reassignment to rubble clearance, evacuation, fleeing or death itself. In October 1943, the MEW reported that Blohm & Voss was experiencing considerable difficulties because of absent workers, and Kaufmann publically appealed for workers

to return. Some 475,000 of the departed 1.2 million people would do so. Many did so because tensions, ranging between indifference and outright hostility, arose between locals and evacuees – complaints from Hamburgers about Bavarians' accent and attitude were frequent – not helped by widespread housing shortages, strict rationing of food, clothes and fuel, and lowering living standards. Mass evacuations caused economic and social stresses throughout Germany, which was, of course, another intended consequence of area bombing.

Those who stayed, observed a Swedish businessman, suffered from 'lack of sleep, a sense of insecurity, and changes in living and factory conditions'. '[N]ervousness and overstrain have served appreciably to reduce industrial effort', it was added, with many engaged in clearing up and repairing damage, and moreover trying to survive. The absence of clean water supplies and efficient refuse collection meant some areas of Hamburg became disease ridden. In February 1944, the MEW noted the city was a 'black spot' with regards to rubbish disposal, with local authorities urging householders to dig disposal pits in lawns and encouraging greater efforts at cleanliness to avoid public health epidemics.

Meanwhile, housing bombed-out populations became problematic, even early in the war. In Hamburg's case, this took a sinister turn in mid-September 1941. Holocaust historian Peter Witte reveals how air raids caused Kaufmann to write immediately to Göring asking for deportation of the city's Jewish population to the Lodz Ghetto to free up dwellings for homeless families. Housing difficulties only worsened as the bombing got heavier, as the British effort at de-housing fully intended. Following *Gomorrah*, a special Commissioner for Housing was appointed to ensure remaining dwelling-space was utilized 'to the fullest extent'. Unpopular practices, particularly doubling-up of families in existing accommodation, were soon introduced. But the shortage remained, further strained by the thousands returning to the city. By late 1943, some 20,000 workers from the Todt Organization were working on prefabricated home construction in Hamburg and the surrounding area, pulled away, of course, from military projects like the Atlantic Wall.

With regards to morale, several senior figures were shaken by the *Gomorrah*[7] attacks. Speer told the Central Planning Committee on 29 July 1943 that 'rapid repetition of this type of attack upon another six German towns would inevitably cripple the will to sustain armaments manufacture and war production', and then '[w]e shall simply be coasting downhill, smoothly and relatively swiftly'.

Adolf Hitler, Führer of Germany from 1933–1945. Although shaken by reports on the bombings, he never visited any German city following an attack, despite being persuaded to by Goebbels and Speer. Only in Berlin was he forced to see it first hand, Speer noted, and 'I saw with what absence of emotion he noted the new areas of rubble through which his car would pass'. Detached to the very end, the destructive war he unleashed on Europe brought untold horror on civilians in cities and towns throughout Germany – as well as for many others right across the Continent. (Getty Images)

---

7   Interviewed by British interrogators, Speer, in that oft-quoted phrase, revealed *Gomorrah* 'made an extraordinary impression' (in his memoirs this became 'Hamburg had put the fear of God in me').

Reconciliation. The Prince of Wales gives a speech in Hamburg during the 50th anniversary of VE Day in May 1995 and laid a wreath at Ohlsdorf Cemetery to the victims of the Allied bombing of Hamburg. Opened in August 1952 as a memorial to the city's 55,000 bombing victims, this beautiful and tranquil cemetery also contains British War Graves from both world wars and a memorial for the victims of the Nazi state. Now, as King Charles III, he visited Hamburg again on 31 March 2023. (Getty Images)

Three days later, he told Hitler that 'a continuation of these attacks might bring about a rapid end to the war' by causing 'a total halt' to armaments production. Hitler merely replied: '[Y]ou'll straighten all that out again.' On 2 August, meeting Hitler and Goebbels, Luftwaffe production supremo Erhard Milch declared 'we have lost the war! Finally lost the war!'. Repeating this to Luftwaffe officers some time later, he added that 'just five or six attacks like these on Hamburg, [and] the German people will just lay down their tools, however great their willpower… What the home front is suffering now cannot be suffered very much longer.' In fact, recent scholarship by Biddle maintains that 'modern industrial societies' have proved 'quite robust, both morally and materially' in the face of aerial bombardment, be it in totalitarian or democratic states, and civilian morale was not susceptible to 'cracking'. Yet evidence from summer 1943 presents a different picture. With the Nazi regime far from concealing Hamburg's destruction, partly because of difficulty in doing so but partly because 'the horrors … were stressed as a means of stirring up a patriotic eagerness for revenge' and recommitment to the war effort, the MEW translated numerous newspaper articles on the morale effect of Hamburg's ordeal. On 31 July, the *Hamburge Zeitung* reported:

> [S]ome people's faith was in danger of being shaken when they saw nothing but destruction and death around them and no help forthcoming – but no human foresight could ever have imagined such a catastrophe and taken the corresponding precautionary defensive measures.

A radio broadcast of Goebbels' 6 August piece in the *Völkischer Beobachter* concluded: 'None of us would like to gloss over the air war against the German homeland. It is putting our nation to a hard test. But we must stand this test. This is one of the prerequisites for victory.' Newspapers beyond Hamburg continued printing articles on the city's ordeal whilst maintaining the line of not giving up. The *Oldenburgische Staatszeitung* wrote: '[I]t would be ridiculous to deny that a terrible nightmare seized many Germans when the reports from Wuppertal and Cologne were followed by the news from Hamburg – but … it is important that the nightmare produces no paralyzing effect.' Certainly, a widespread sense of impending doom did grip Germany during summer 1943. Like similar port cities and shipbuilding centres, it was written that the civilian mood in Bremen 'not unnaturally seems to have reacted sharply to the Hamburg attacks', whilst Stettin was consumed by 'manifest apprehension' about sharing Hamburg's fate. Above all, the atmosphere in Berlin verged on complete panic, strongly tinged with anti-regime feeling. On 13 August 1943, the Berlin correspondent for the Swedish newspaper *Svenska Morgenpost* wrote:

> [T]he bitterness of the people turned against the Nazi Government, which is regarded as responsible for the unspeakable misery. The general feeling is: Hitler started total war but the British are carrying it out… [It was] becoming increasingly difficult to believe in a German victory.

Ultra decrypted an account by the Turkish Ambassador in Berlin informing Ankara that bombing 'might lead eventually to the internal collapse of Germany', with anti-party slogans being chalked on walls and 'defacement of pictures of Hitler to the accompaniment of extremely coarse language'. Evidence from the time led the British to believe serious inroads had been made into German morale, which was rebounding on the regime's popularity. Throughout August 1943, the RAF dropped 35.5 million copies of a leaflet titled 'This was

Hamburg'. Featuring a large photograph of the devastation, this reflected the strategy of the Political Warfare Executive, a covert British propaganda service, to engender panic and mass movement of the population from towns and cities to undermine German war production.

Yet the Nazi regime – and Germany's war-effort – not only weathered the summer 1943 crisis but continued for another 18 months. Using 'unprecedented number[s] of injunctions against rumour-mongering' and those 'relating sensational stories in shelters during air attacks', mere signs of flagging morale was checked by the German authorities through legal action, punishments or, as reported in mid-August, deployment in Berlin of 60,000 SS personnel to assist in maintaining control. Mark Clodfelter assesses that airpower, whether selective or indiscriminate, 'could not shred the tightly-woven fabric of complete subservience that comprised Nazi Germany … [which proved] simply too strong for a single episode to destroy the nation's collective resolve to keep fighting'. After the war, Harris acknowledged bombing to break civilian morale was a 'totally unsound' proposition because 'when we had destroyed almost all the large industrial cities in Germany the civil population remained apathetic, while the Gestapo saw to it that they were docile, and in so far as there was work for them to do, industrious'. Bombing was destructive and likely to create short-term despondency, but it never caused German society to crack fully. '[If] defined as their will to continue to work for the war effort, then German moral was not broken', Horst Boog observes, although 'it was certainly weakened'. But he added:

Like Coventry cathedral, the monument to the bombing of Hamburg is the partially destroyed St Nikolai Kirche. (Getty Images)

> People continued to do their duty in a fatalistic and apathetic mood, and this did not increase their devotion to the political cause and to productivity. It was not morale in this sense that kept them on the ball. Rather it was the desire to survive – which, under the circumstances of the political surveillance system, also meant doing what one was told and not shirking in the presence of others.

On 19 October 1943, the RE8 (Research and Experiments) department of the MoHS (Ministry of Home Security) reported on how much British raids had affected Germany's industrial production between July and September. On average, all towns had lost 'some 3 weeks' production', the Ruhr 'probably' four to six weeks and Hamburg and Remscheid the most at 11 weeks. The USSBS study on the effects of area attacks on Hamburg put the figure lower at 1.8 months, the product of an immediate 50 per cent drop in industrial production during August, but the output figure increasing to 82 per cent of its usual total during the rest of 1943 in a seemingly impressive recovery. Yet the industrial requirements of fighting *Totaler Krieg* (Total War) meant any significant reduction carried implications. The American report, wondering what 'the comparative effect of the area and precision raids would have been' if the former had been 'repeated over a longer period', concluded that area attacks *had* 'already wiped out most of the city's surplus production capacity before the precision attacks started'. The US Eighth's heavy attacks in 1944 thus commenced when Hamburg's production was already under strain. As historian Adam Tooze explains, expanded no further, the Americans' precision bombing ate into the remaining productive capacity existing in Hamburg (like many other places), and area bombing had therefore played an important role in setting distinct limits on the city's war economy.

From May 1940, the beautiful Hanseatic port city of Hamburg was bombed right to the bitter end of the war, transformed into the devastated urban landscape that Bufton, Trenchard and others observed from the air in May and June 1945. Many cities suffered appallingly from aerial bombardment during World War II, but Hamburg's experience was one of the worst, perpetrated in a war that was itself full of excesses.

FURTHER READING

Cited here are some of the original documents, official accounts, books and articles that have been used for writing this book.

Archival Sources

The National Archives (TNA), Kew
Files in AIR2, AIR14, AIR20, AIR22, AIR24, AIR41, AIR48, AIR69

Churchill Archives Centre, Cambridge
Bufton Papers: Files 3/27, 3/36, 3/51, 3/65

Archive Collection, RAF Museum, Hendon
Harris Papers: Files H13, H19, H28, H40, H101, H105

British Online Archives (https://microform.digital/boa/)
FO837 (M.E.W. Weekly Intelligence Reports)

Official Histories, Reports, Diaries & Memoirs

Air Ministry, The Rise and Fall of the German Air Force (TNA, 2008ed.)

Boog H., et al, Germany and the Second World War, Vol. VII, 1943–1944/5 (OUP, 2015ed.),

BBSU, The Strategic Air War Against Germany 1939–1945: The Official Report of the British Bombing Survey Unit (Frank Cass, 1998)

Charlwood, D., No Moon Tonight (Goodall, 1990ed.)

Gibson, G., Enemy Coast Ahead (Greenhill, 2019ed.)

Greenhous, B., et al, The Crucible of War: The Official History of the Royal Canadian Air Force, Volume III (University of Toronto Press, 1994)

Harris, A., Dispatch on War Operations (Frank Cass, 1995)

Harris, A., Bomber Offensive (Pen & Sword, 2005ed.)

Herrmann, H., Eagle's Wings: The Autobiography of a Luftwaffe Pilot (Airlife, 1991)

Isby, D. (ed.), Fighting the Bombers: The Luftwaffe's struggle against the Allied Bomber Offensive (Greenhill, 2003)

Johnen, H., Duel Under the Stars: The Memoir of a Luftwaffe Night Pilot in World War II (Greenhill, 2020ed.)

Jones, R.V., Most Secret War: British Scientific Intelligence 1939–1945 (Penguin, 2009ed.)

Knoke, H., I flew For The Führer: The Memoirs of a Luftwaffe Fighter Pilot (Greenhill, 2012ed.)

Roskill, S., The War At Sea 1939–45; vol. II: The Period of Balance (HMSO, 1954)

Sawyer, T., Only Owls and Bloody Fools Fly at Night (Goodall, 2000ed.)

Spoden, P., Enemy in the Dark: The Story of a Luftwaffe Night-Fighter Pilot (Private, 2003)

Trevor-Roper, H. (ed.), The Goebbels Diaries (Secker & Warburg, 1978)

Thompson, W.R., Lancaster to Berlin (Goodall, 1997)

Von Below, N., At Hitler's Side: The Memoirs of Hitler's Luftwaffe Adjutant 1937–1945 (Greenhill, 2001)

Von Müllenheim-Rechberg, Baron B., Battleship Bismarck: A Survivor's Story (Triad/Panther, 1982),

Webster C./Frankland N., The Strategic Air Offensive against Germany 1939–1945, vol. I-IV (HMSO, 1961)

Books

Bekker, C., *Luftwaffe War Diaries: The German Air Force in World War II* (Da Capo, 1994ed.)

Buckley, J., *Air Power in the Age of Total War* (UCL Press, 1999)

Davis-Biddle, T., *Rhetoric and Reality in Air Warfare: The Evolution of British and American Ideas about Strategic Bombing*, 1914–1945 (Princeton, 2004ed.)

Everitt C./Middlebrook M., *Bomber Command War Diaries, 1939–1945* (Midland, 1998)

Hastings, M., *Bomber Command* (Pan, 2007ed.)

Hinchcliffe, P., *The Other Battle: Luftwaffe Night Aces Versus Bomber Command* (Airlife, 1996)

Lambert, M., *Night After Night: New Zealanders in Bomber Command* (HarperCollins, 2007)

Lowe, K., Inferno: *The Devastation of Hamburg* (Penguin, 2008)

Middlebrook M., *Battle for Hamburg: The Firestorm Raid* (Cassell, 2000ed.)

Murray, W., *Strategy for Defeat: The Luftwaffe 1939–1945* (Air University Press, 1983)

Overy, R., *The Bombing War: Europe 1939–1945* (Allen Lane, 2013)

Probert, H., *Bomber Harris: His Life and Times* (Greenhill, 2006)

Richards, D., *RAF Bomber Command in the Second World War: The Hardest Victory* (Penguin, 2001)

Tooze, A. *The Wages of Destruction: The Making and Breaking of the Nazi War Economy* (Penguin, 2007)

Wilson, K., *Bomber Boys: The Ruhr, Dambusters and Bloody Berlin* (Cassell, 2006)

INDEX

Page numbers in **bold** refer to illustrations and their captions.